On Eagles' Wings

Hershel Brand

On Eagles' Wings

Moshiach, Redemption, and the World to Come

Hershel Brand

TARGUM/FELDHEIM

First published 2002
Copyright © 2002 by Hershel Brand
ISBN 1-56871-214-6

Published by:
Targum Press, Inc.
22700 W. Eleven Mile Rd.
Southfield, MI 48034
E-mail: targum@netvision.net.il
Fax: 888-298-9992
www.targum.com

Distributed by:
Feldheim Publishers
202 Airport Executive Park
Nanuet, NY 10954
www.feldheim.com

Printed in Israel

Rabbi Aharon Feldman

409 Yeshiva Lane
Baltimore, MD 21208
Rosh HaYeshiva, Yeshivas Ner Israel

בס״ד, ירושלים, כח באב תשס״ב

Since the belief in Moshiach is one of the cardinal principles of Judaism, it is obviously incumbent upon us to be clear about what this belief entails. By defining the concept of Moshiach as it is understood by the classic sources for English speaking readers, "On Eagles' Wings" is an important contribution towards the attainment of this clairty.

Particularly in our times, to define who Moshiach is not, is as vital as to define who he is. The concept of Moshiach has in recent years been perverted by irresponsible elements of Jewry by the introduction of foreign concepts; for example, that the Moshiach will be resurrected from the dead or, alternatively, that he is an embodiment of the Divine. Your book shows that these concepts have no basis in Jewish *mesorah* (tradition).

May your book bring the Jewish people closer to true *emunah* (faith), and may we be worthy to witness the coming of Moshiach speedily in our days.

With the blessings of the Torah,

Aharon Feldman

Rabbi Zev Leff

Rabbi of Moshav Matityahu
Rosh Hayeshiva Yeshiva Gedola Matisyahu
d.n. moddiin 71917 tel. (08) 976-1138 fax. (08) 976-5326

I have read the manuscript of "On Eagles' Wings" by Rabbi Hershel Brand שליט״א. The author presents a comprehensive study of the concept of Moshiach and the various issues pertaining to this principle of faith.

This presentation also includes the significance and implications of awaiting anxiously the coming of Moshiach, and the effect it must have on one's outlook on life in general. The Rambam says that the details of this topic are obscure and were not revealed neither to the prophets in the written Torah nor to the sages in the oral Torah. Therefore, due to this obscurity much confusion exists concerning Moshiach and many misconceptions and distortions have developed.

The author presents a very lucid, detailed discussion that gives one a solid understanding of the various oppinions as to what is entatiled in belief of Moshiach. The format utilized, a discussion between Rabbi and student, (following the style of Rav Yehudah HaLevi in the Kuzari) is very effective and contributes to the understanding of the issues.

I recommend this work to Yeshivah students and laymen alike since the information contained in it is crucial to one's full belief and understanding of this principle of faith.

May the author be blessed with life, health, and prosperity enabling him to continue to merit the community with further works of Torah.

With Torah blessings
Sincerely,

Rabbi Zev Leff

On Eagles' Wings

is dedicated *l'iluy nishmas*

our beloved mother

רחל חוה בת יוסף בנימין ע״ה

נפטרה ה׳ חשון תשל״ו

ת.נ.צ.ב.ה

Contents

Acknowledgments

This book could not have been written without the generous assistance of many colleagues and friends, and I thank you all. Several deserve particular mention.

Words cannot express my gratitude to my *rosh yeshivah*, Rav Binyomin Moskovits, *shlita*. Rarely a day passes that I don't recall some Torah wisdom that I learned at his feet. He is a giant in both Torah and *chesed*, and this book is the direct result of his encouragement and support over the years.

I am deeply grateful to the entire Ner Yaakov family and Rabbi Yehoshua Liff in particular. His boundless energy and enthusiasm for spreading the message of Torah has been a great personal motivation. He believed in me enough to make me part of the Ner Yaakov experience, and he continues to provide me with the opportunity to express my love for teaching and learning Torah. May God grant him, his family, and the yeshivah long, happy, and successful years.

Words cannot express my gratitude to the *rosh yeshivah* of Ner Yisrael, HaRav Aharon Feldman, *shlita*. Not only did he review the entire manuscipt (twice!) and offer many practical suggestions, comments, and corrections, but he also graciously wrote a special letter of *berachah* to the *sefer*.

I am deeply grateful to Rabbi Moshe Shapiro, *shlita*, who generously answered my numerous, difficult questions concerning the complex subjects of this book.

I would like to give special thanks to Mrs. Jackie Hecht. Aside from the continual love and support that she has given over the years, her help was instrumental in the publication of this book.

I am deeply grateful to my brother, Rabbi David Brand. A person often feels pressured to emulate the success of elder siblings. His dedication, wisdom, and determination in all matters of Torah and mitzvos make him a hard act to follow. I have always looked to him and his *rebbetzin* as a perfect example of how a *frum ba'al habayis* can achieve greatness in all aspects of life. The publication of this book would not have been possible without his generous support. Also, despite the burdens of business and family, he took the time to review the manuscript and offer excellent advice and practical suggestions. May Hashem reward their kindness and dedication with long and happy years of health and *nachas*.

I wish to publicly express my thanks to Rabbi Zev Cohen, Rabbi Dovid Zaltzbacher, and Rabbi Yosef Brown, all of whom had a serious impact on my Torah development and growth as a person. May they be *zocheh* to inspire legions of new *talmidim*.

My sincere and heartfelt appreciation is extended to Rabbi Adam Schwartz, Binyomin Levkov, Yonasan Stern, and Yisroel Moshe Rosenberg for reviewing the manuscript and their insightful comments and suggestions.

A warm thanks to Rabbi Chananya Greenwald. A source of great inspiration and advice over the years, he helped me obtain answers to my most difficult "Moshiach" problems at a critical juncture.

A special thanks to Russ Shulkes, whose support was crucial to the publication of this book. Additionally, he reviewed the entire manuscript and offered many practical suggestions.

I wish to thank Rabbi Aharon Lopian for his invaluable guidance and constant moral support.

Words cannot express my debt of gratitude to Rabbi Avraham Edelstein. The credit for this book's existence goes to him as much as myself, since the idea was originally his own. He is a leader of men and a builder of Torah institutions, yet the "smaller" kindness that he showed my family personally proves his true greatness as an individual.

A special thanks to Rabbi Kenneth and Esti Berger and Dr. Israel and Minna Berger for their generous contribution toward the publication of this work. I especially appreciate the many years of ongoing frienship and familial warmth.

I wish to thank Rav Yosef Kamenetsky, who graciously spent an entire hectic *erev Shabbos* answering my numerous questions.

A special thanks to D. Liff, for the awe-inspiring cover design and layout.

I also want to thank my in-laws, Reb Yisrael and Shaindel Zimmer, for their ongoing encouragement and support.

Finally, I would like to take this opportunity to express my deep appreciation for the constant support and assistance I have received from my wife, Suri. She was the first reader, editor, and proofreader of this work, and the imprint of her acute literary skills and penetrating intellect can be felt on every page. What is mine is hers in all things, and in this book in particular.

Introduction

One problem inherent to learning about the Moshiach, the War of Gog U'Magog, Eliyahu HaNavi, and the World to Come is that there is no *"masseches Moshiach."* There is no single gathering place in Talmudic literature for the many statements Chazal made concerning these concepts. One who wishes to learn about these subjects is forced to search far and wide before he can piece together a viable picture. Of course, Rav Sa'adyah Gaon and some *Rishonim*, such as the Rambam, the Ramban, and the Abarbanel, did discuss these topics, and it is through them that we fully understand the meaning of Chazal's aggadic discussions. But it is still a great undertaking to sift carefully through their words. And this, of course, is true only for those who comprehend the original language of the sources. For those who cannot, the world of the Moshiach is practically closed.

But there is a greater, if more subtle, problem involved. Chazal say: "Rabbi Yehudah used to say: A person should always digest words of Torah as general principles and reproduce them as details, as it says, 'May my teachings drop like rain...' " (*Sifri, Devarim* 32:2).

The Ramchal, in the introduction to *Derech Hashem*, explains that when a person is confronted by a plethora of details about a subject but does not understand how the details interrelate, he is practically lost. Since he has no idea how the specific pieces fit together, he has a difficult time visualizing the whole. On the other hand, when a person understands a general concept, he can automatically apply that knowledge to a great variety of details. He can even figure out the details for himself.

Imagine you and a friend are exploring a junkyard, when you come upon a great heap of auto parts. You know little about the inner workings of a car, so it seems to be just a jumble of random parts. Your friend, however, is an expert mechanic and points out and names each part — a spark plug, a gasket, a piston — and explains its function. Yet even when he's finished, you still have no idea how this pile of metal provides locomotion. In order to understand how a car runs, you have to first look at a running engine. It's only when you see the big picture, how the pieces interrelate, that you can begin to disassemble the engine and appreciate the individual details.

These words of the Ramchal help us understand why most people know very little about the concepts of the Moshiach and the World to Come. There is a lot of information available on these subjects but very little explanation of its meaning.

Everyone knows a few details. You might know that the Moshiach will arrive as soon as the Jewish people repent. You might know that Eliyahu is supposed to arrive before the Moshiach. You might have heard that there will be not one but two resurrections of the dead. But these are all merely details. They don't reach the core of the issues. In order to really understand these complex subjects (and the same is true with every Torah subject), a person must first understand the underlying principles. Only then will the details become clear.

The emphasis of this book is to convey an understanding of the ideas behind the concept of the Moshiach rather than the details. We will talk about the two resurrections of the dead, but only after we discuss why we need to be resurrected. We will discuss the question of what the Moshiach must accomplish, but first we'll explain why we need a Moshiach in the first place.

There are many ways to write a book, and I pondered how to present this information for an inordinate amount of time. Finally I settled on Socratic dialogue, a record of a discussion between two people, in this case a rabbi and his student. It is the same approach the Ramchal used in *Da'as Tevunos* and Rabbi Yehudah HaLevi in the *Kuzari*.

The primary disadvantage to this method is that, in addition to the care that goes into the material, I must also be concerned with the dialogue of the characters. It must flow as an actual conversation, yet retain focus on the subject at hand. But the conversation can be more interesting than a dry treatise, and it can help to bring a somewhat complex subject down to earth. It's no coincidence that *Da'as Tevunos* and the *Kuzari* both discuss relatively involved, theoretical matters.

When I first began studying the subject of Moshiach more than three years ago, I never dreamed it would evolve into a project of this magnitude. A wise teacher once told me that usually God need only nudge a person in the right direction. But occasionally God's guidance is both miraculous and overt, and that was certainly the case here. I hope that *On Eagles' Wings* teaches and inspires the reader as much as it taught and inspired me. And I pray that God brings the Moshiach and redemption speedily and in our days.

How to Use
This Book Effectively

Those who, like myself, tend to skip instructions and dive into a task, probably won't be reading this section. But for those who prefer a bit of guidance, I offer the following.

The book was purposely written in a way that it can be enjoyed on many levels. If you wish to gain a full and complete understanding of the Moshiach, the resurrection of the dead, and the World to Come, simply read through the conversation between Rabbi Cohen and Daniel, ignoring the indented sources that are sprinkled liberally throughout the text.

For skeptics who wish to see proof of the statements, or those who would just like a deeper understanding of the subject, I recommend they read the indented sources.

Finally, if you wish to gain an even deeper level of understanding and enjoy tangential discussions, I suggest that you read Rabbi Cohen's notes, which have been fully reproduced after the final chapter.

Prologue

One afternoon Rabbi Cohen finds Daniel sitting in a corner of the *beis midrash*, frowning at a large stack of *sefarim*.

RABBI COHEN: Is everything all right?

DANIEL: Yes...I mean, no. I was studying the Rambam's thirteen principles of faith this morning, and I realized that I know next to nothing about one of the principles — the obligation to await the arrival of the Moshiach. I've been doing research all morning, but nothing I've found makes sense to me. It's like trying to assemble a puzzle with only half the pieces.

Here's an example. The Rambam says that the Moshiach himself will rebuild the Beis HaMikdash. Okay, I thought. That sounds pretty straightforward. Then someone told me that the third Beis HaMikdash is already built in Heaven and will descend to its place when the redemption arrives.

> In the future, the Moshiach will...rebuild the Beis HaMikdash.
>
> (Rambam, *Hilchos Melachim* 11:1)

However, the future Mikdash that we await is already built and completed; it will fall from the Heavens, as it says, "The Sanctuary, my Lord, which Your hands established" (*Shemos* 15:17).

(*Rashi, Sukkah* 41a, s.v. "*iy nami*")

So which is it? One of them has to be right. But it's much more than that. I don't really understand what the Moshiach is all about. Who is he? When is he coming? Why do we need him anyway? I'm very confused.

RABBI COHEN: I can certainly understand your confusion. Sometimes the subject perplexes me, too.

DANIEL: It does?

RABBI COHEN: Of course. After all, the Rambam also wrote that although the Sages teach us about the Moshiach, much of the truth will remain hidden until the events actually take place. And since the Sages knew about the era of the Moshiach only from their insight into the verses that discuss it, they disagreed about some of the specifics.

> And in all these things [the concept of the Moshiach and the details of his arrival], no one knows for certain what will take place until it actually occurs, because these things were left cryptic by the prophets. The Sages also had no specific tradition regarding these matters except for what they could understand of the passages [in Tanach that discuss the Moshiach]. Therefore the Sages disagreed about certain aspects of these matters.
>
> (Rambam, *Hilchos Melachim* 12:2)

DANIEL: Great. Now there's really no hope. If the concept of the Moshiach was unclear to the Sages, what chance do I have to ever understand it?

RABBI COHEN: Well, the situation is not all that grim. I just mean to show you that no matter how deeply you delve into the subject, there will always remain points that are impossible to predict. But I think you might be surprised at how much the Sages really understood from verses in Tanach. A research physicist, for example, might tell you that he doesn't truly understand super-string theory. Yet he would certainly be able to teach a class in advanced physics.

DANIEL: But if the Sages argued about so many points, how much can we really know about the subject? Who's going to rebuild the Beis HaMikdash? It's a *machlokes*. How will the Moshiach arrive? It's a *machlokes*. It's all disagreements.

RABBI COHEN: It's true that the Sages disagreed about some of these ideas, though less than you probably think. However, it's often the disagreements themselves that grant us the greatest insight.

DANIEL: The disagreements themselves? Now I'm really confused.

RABBI COHEN: I mean that when we examine the disagreements closely, it becomes clear that they agreed on many underlying points and themes. Coupled with facts that are universally agreed on, there is much that we can understand about the Moshiach.

DANIEL: I see...sort of. But doesn't it say that —

RABBI COHEN: I'll tell you what, Daniel. Why don't we sit down once a week to learn about the subject in detail?

DANIEL: Really? That would be great.

RABBI COHEN: There's just one thing I want you to do before next week.

DANIEL: Homework already?

RABBI COHEN: Not exactly. I merely want you to write down every question you have on the topic of the Moshiach and the period of his arrival. Next week we'll start at the top of your list and work our way down.

DANIEL: No problem. But don't say you weren't warned. I've got tons of questions.

RABBI COHEN: So much the better. I'll see you next week.

Week 1

In which Daniel learns why the Jewish nation needs a Moshiach

RABBI COHEN: Did you prepare your list?

DANIEL: You bet. At first I thought I would ask you what the Moshiach is supposed to do once he gets here. Then I realized that I don't even understand why he's coming in the first place. I mean, God already gave the Torah to the Jewish nation; He already told us what He expects from us. What is the world lacking? Why do we need a Moshiach?

RABBI COHEN: An excellent question and a fine place to start. Rabbi Moshe Chaim Luzzato, the Ramchal, explains that as part of God's ultimate plan the world and creation at large must reach a state of perfection. That cannot happen, however, until the Jewish people themselves reach their optimal state. The purpose of the Moshiach is to bring the Jewish nation close to God and to assist it in all ways to attain the requisite perfection. In turn, the entire creation will become sanctified and perfected. In essence, the Moshiach is the instrument through which the world will fulfill its destiny.

> You must know that even though true good is acquired by each person according to his deeds, creation as a whole cannot be perfected until the entire chosen nation exists in its optimum

state. They must be perfected through every possible aspect, and the Divine Presence must attach itself to them. Subsequently the entire world will be able to attain a perfect state, and each person will attain what he earned according to his deeds....

The Highest Wisdom set a time limit for the effort of man and his quest for perfection to six thousand years. After that time the world will be renewed in a different form, appropriate to its ultimate destiny, which is the eternal pleasure of those people who merit it. Before this six-thousand-year period comes to an end, the chosen nation must attain perfection in order that the world can be transformed into its final state.

We have been guaranteed that this will take place no matter what happens. The catalyst for this will be a descendant of King David, whom God will choose specifically for this task and help him to succeed. This person will be the Moshiach.

(Ramchal, *Ma'amar Halkarim, "BaGeulah"*)

DANIEL: That makes sense. But it only partially answers the question. Why can't the Jewish nation achieve perfection on its own?

RABBI COHEN: The Rambam tells us that the reason we hope for the arrival of the Moshiach is not so that we can eat, drink, and be merry. I would say that's probably the most common misconception about the Moshiach. Nor do we desire the arrival of the Moshiach so that we can rule over the gentiles or take revenge on them for past faults. Rather, we await the Moshiach in order that we will be able to concentrate on learning Torah and serving God without distraction.

In other words, the Rambam is telling us that the Moshiach will assist the Jewish nation to do what it is supposed to be doing anyway — studying the Torah and serving God. Unfortunately, the current state of exile hampers the Jewish nation. The constant wars, oppression, and myriad forms of misery we experience in exile distract us from our goal. By removing all the elements of the exile, the Moshiach will allow us to focus our energy once more on attaining a state of perfection. And, as I said before, when the Jewish people attain perfection, the entire creation will reach its destiny.

> The prophets and the Sages did not desire the days of the Moshiach in order to rule the world, to persecute the nations, to be exalted by the nations, or to eat, drink, and be merry. Rather, they desired the arrival of the Moshiach in order that they would be free to concentrate on the Torah and its wisdom without oppression or disruption, in order to merit life in the World to Come.
>
> (Rambam, *Hilchos Melachim* 12:4)

DANIEL: All right, I think I understand the idea. Can you tell me anything specific that the Moshiach will do?

RABBI COHEN: Of course. Though once you understand the underlying idea, you'll be able to guess many of them anyway.

DANIEL: Like gathering the exiles.

RABBI COHEN: Exactly. One of the first tasks of the Moshiach will be to bring every Jew to Eretz Yisrael. This concept is mentioned explicitly in both the Torah and the Prophets.

> Hashem, your God, will return your captivity and have mercy upon you, and He will return and gather you in from all the peoples to which Hashem your God has scattered you. If your dispersed will be at the ends of heaven, from there Hashem, your God, will gather you in, and from there He will take you.

Hashem, your God, will bring you to the land that your forefathers inherited, and you shall inherit it.

(Devarim 30:3–5)

He will gather the castaways of Israel, and He will assemble the dispersed ones of Yehudah from the four corners of the earth.

(Yeshayah 11:12)

Therefore, behold, days are coming, says God, when people will no longer say, "the Living God, Who brought the children of Israel up from the land of Egypt," but rather, "the Living God, Who brought up and returned the offspring of the House of Israel from the land of the north and from all the lands wherein He had dispersed them," and they will return to their own land.

(Yirmeyah 23:7–8)

Along the same lines, once the Jewish nation returns to Eretz Yisrael, the Moshiach will also reestablish the Jewish kingdom, with himself as king.

The original kingdom will return, the kingdom of the daughter of Jerusalem.

(Michah 4:8)

In the future the Moshiach will arise and reestablish the kingdom of the House of David to its original rulership.

(Rambam, *Hilchos Melachim* 11:1)

DANIEL: When the Jewish people last had a king, wasn't the nation actually divided into two separate kingdoms, Yisrael and Yehudah?

RABBI COHEN: Correct. The Moshiach, however, will rule over a unified Jewish nation.

And I will make them into one nation in the land, upon the

mountains of Israel, and one king will rule over them all; they will no longer be two nations, and they will not be divided into two kingdoms ever again.

(Yechezkel 37:22)

Can you think of any other tasks that fit with our theme of the Moshiach giving the Jewish nation a chance to concentrate on their service to God?

DANIEL: Well, the Moshiach would also have to protect the Jewish people from enemies.

RABBI COHEN: Correct. A nation that is being oppressed can hardly function at full capacity. Therefore the Moshiach will also protect the Jewish people from any harm.

DANIEL: Hmmm...no disrespect intended, but how exactly is that going to happen? Even if we assume that the Moshiach will be a political genius, how will he protect the Jewish nation from an enemy that insists on attacking us? Do you mean that he will raise a massive army or invent some sort of new weapon or defense shield? I assume he's not going to go out and fight them single-handedly.

RABBI COHEN: Not at all. Remember that the Moshiach has friends in high places. In fact, the Moshiach will not even have to wage conventional warfare against the enemies of the Jewish nation.[1]

This will be the plague with which God will strike all the peoples that have gathered against Jerusalem: Each one's flesh will melt away while he is standing on his feet, each one's eyes will melt away in their sockets, and each one's tongue will melt away in their mouths.

(Zechariah 14:12)

Among the wonders attributed to the Moshiach is that he will fight his wars without exertion and destroy his enemies with neither sword nor spear. This difference is attributed to the Moshiach, as it says, "He will strike [the wicked] of the world with the rod of his mouth, and with the breath of his lips he will slay the wicked" (*Yeshayah* 11:4), which the Sages explained applies to the War of Gog U'Magog.[2]

(Abarbanel, *Yeshuos Meshicho* 1:3)

The Ramban compares this aspect of the Moshiach to that of Moshe Rabbeinu, who single-handedly defeated Egypt, a superpower of the ancient world. You can imagine how Pharaoh and his court must have laughed when Moshe and Aharon, two elderly men, came to the palace with the demand that Egypt free an entire population of slaves. But they weren't laughing for long. The Moshiach will defeat today's world powers in the same way.

The Moshiach will not fight with armies or might, but rather with his spirit, which trusts in God. Similarly [Moshe] the original savior came with his staff and his haversack to Pharaoh and defeated his country with the rod of his mouth.

(Ramban, *Kisvei HaRamban*, vol. 1, p. 322)

DANIEL: I assume the Moshiach will also act as a teacher of the Jewish people.

RABBI COHEN: Of course. Ultimately that is the primary way in which the Moshiach will influence the Jewish nation — as a teacher and spiritual mentor. And, according to the Rambam, this is one of the ways to identify a potential Moshiach. Before we recognize a person as the Moshiach, he must be wise in all aspects of the Torah and influence the entire Jewish people to keep the Torah and do *teshuvah*. There are other necessary qualifications, but we can discuss those at another time.

> And if a king of the House of David, who is versed in Torah and occupied with mitzvos as David his ancestor, in both the Written Torah and the Oral Law, rises and influences the entire Jewish people to walk in the [Torah's] path and strengthen their observance...we can assume he is the Moshiach.
>
> (Rambam, *Hilchos Melachim* 11:4)

And while it's true that the Moshiach's primary task will be to bring the Jewish nation closer to God, the Moshiach will also convince the entire world of the existence of God and the truth of the Torah.

> It will happen in the end of days that the mountain of the Temple of God will be firmly established as the highest of the mountains and be exalted above the hills, and all the nations will stream to it. Many peoples will go and say, "Come, let us go up to the Mountain of God, to the Temple of the God of Yaakov, and he [the Moshiach] will teach us His ways, and we will walk in His paths." For from Zion the Torah will go forth and the Word of God from Jerusalem.
>
> (*Yeshayah* 2:2–3)

> For then I will change the nations to [speak] a pure language, to call upon the Name of God, to serve Him with united resolve.
>
> (*Tzefaniah* 3:9)

> Therefore [the Moshiach] will instruct the entire [Jewish] people and teach them the way of God, and all of the nations will come to listen....
>
> (Rambam, *Hilchos Teshuvah* 9:2)

DANIEL: Is there anything else?

RABBI COHEN: Most of the remaining tasks of the Moshiach are related to the reinstitution of the mitzvos. In exile, the Jewish nation is able to keep only a portion of the 613 commandments. Since the coming of the Moshiach heralds our return to the Land of Israel and the rebuilding of the Beis HaMikdash, we will again merit to keep every mitzvah. Clearly the rebuilding of the Beis HaMikdash will be one of the Moshiach's first tasks.

> The Moshiach, who was placed in the north, will arrive and build the Beis HaMikdash, which was placed in the south.
>
> (*Midrash Rabbah, Vayikra* 9:6)

> In the future, the Moshiach will...rebuild the Beis HaMikdash.
>
> (Rambam, *Hilchos Melachim* 11:1)

DANIEL: So you're saying that the Moshiach will be responsible for rebuilding the Beis HaMikdash. That's what I always thought. But, like I said last week, someone told me that the third Beis HaMikdash is fully built in Heaven. When the Moshiach arrives, it will descend to its place down here. So which is it?

> However, the future Mikdash that we await is already built and completed; it will fall from the Heavens, as it says, "The Sanctuary, my Lord, which Your hands established" (*Shemos* 15:17).
>
> (*Rashi, Sukkah* 41a, s.v. "*iy nami*")

RABBI COHEN: That's an excellent question, and I will tackle it in two ways. First, the *Aruch L'Ner* suggests that the two *midrashim* are not contradictory at all. Although the Moshiach will rebuild the "body" of the Beis HaMikdash — the stones and mortar that compose its physical structure — the "soul" of the Beis HaMikdash, its intangible spiritual component, will descend from Heaven.

> Therefore, in my humble opinion, the Beis HaMikdash of the future will be a real building constructed by man. The verse "The Sanctuary, my Lord, that Your hands established" (*Shemos* 15:17), which the *Midrash Tanchuma* explains [as referring to

the Beis HaMikdash of the future, which] will descend from above, is referring to a spiritual Beis HaMikdash, which will enter the physical Beis HaMikdash as a soul resides in its body....

(*Aruch L'Ner, Sukkah* 41a, s.v. *"sham divrei hamaschil iy nami"*)

DANIEL: That's a fascinating idea.

RABBI COHEN: I agree. And the comparison to a human soul is particularly apt. A person might live his entire life without ever recognizing that he has a soul, yet that is precisely what makes him alive. So, too, the Beis HaMikdash appears as a building composed of stones and cement. However, it also contains a deeper, inner aspect that brings it "alive." This "soul" is the Beis HaMikdash that is already prepared in Heaven.

DANIEL: So what's the second answer?

RABBI COHEN: I think we'll hold off on that for a little while.

DANIEL: I have a feeling I'll be hearing that a lot.

RABBI COHEN: I can understand your impatience, but there's an important concept we need to discuss first. Don't worry. I promise we'll get back to it.

DANIEL: Okay.

RABBI COHEN: So, as we were saying, the Moshiach will rebuild the Beis HaMikdash. Now, in order that we can know who is supposed to serve in what capacity in the Beis HaMikdash, the Moshiach will also determine which tribe every Jew belongs to. He will determine the legitimacy of each Kohen and Levi.

During the days of the Moshiach, when his kingdom has become established and he has gathered the entire Jewish nation, he will classify their lineage using the *ruach hakodesh* [divine inspiration] that rests upon him.... However, the Moshiach will classify them only according to which tribe they belong....

(Rambam, *Hilchos Melachim* 12:3)

And the remainder of the mitzvos that we don't fulfill presently, such as the mitzvos of *shemittah* and *yovel*, and the reinstitution of the *Sanhedrin* will also return during the time of the Moshiach.

In the future...all the courts will operate as they did originally, and they will observe the *shemittah* and *yovel* like all mitzvos mentioned in the Torah.

(Rambam, *Hilchos Melachim* 11:1)

DANIEL: All right, it's very clear now. Let me try to sum up what we've learned so far. In order for God's plans for creation to be realized, the Jewish nation must first reach a state of complete holiness and perfection. However, the trials and tribulations of the exile distract and prevent them from attaining this goal. By ending the exile, the Moshiach — king, teacher, and spiritual mentor — will be the catalyst that will ensure the Jewish people attain perfection.

The rebuilding of the Beis HaMikdash, the restoration of the *Sanhedrin*, and the reinstitution of certain mitzvos of the Torah are all tasks the Moshiach will accomplish as part of the ultimate plan of bringing the Jewish nation to perfection.

RABBI COHEN: Beautiful. I couldn't have said it better myself. You see? It's not all that difficult to understand.

DANIEL: Ah, but you haven't heard my next question.

RABBI COHEN: I think we've learned enough for one day. Save your question, and we'll deal with it first thing next week.

DANIEL: Terrific. I'll see you then.

Week 2

In which Daniel learns how to identify the true Moshiach

DANIEL: All right, this time I'm positive you'll be stumped.

RABBI COHEN: Luckily I never claimed to be all-knowing. Try me and we'll see.

DANIEL: Someone once told me that each and every generation has a Moshiach.

RABBI COHEN: I think what he meant was that each generation has a person who is righteous enough to become the Moshiach. That doesn't make him the redeemer, only a potential candidate. When God decides the time is right, that person's inherent potential will be actualized. The Jewish nation will not have to wait all the time it would take for a savior to be born and raised. When the time arrives, that person will become the Moshiach and redeem the Jewish people immediately.

> In every generation there is a person who is fitting to be the Moshiach if the generation merits it.
>
> (*Pri Tzaddik, Devarim* 13)

> Immediately following the destruction of the Beis HaMikdash a person was born who, by virtue of his righteousness, was

fitting to be the redeemer. When the set time arrives, God will appear to him and send him....

(Chasam Sofer, Responsa, vol. 6, 98, s.v. "hareini nazir")

DANIEL: So here's my question: If the Moshiach is alive today, just who exactly is he?

RABBI COHEN: You're right. I can't answer the question.

DANIEL: I knew it.

RABBI COHEN: But do you understand *why* I can't answer the question?

DANIEL: Uh...because it would spoil these learning sessions?

RABBI COHEN: Nice try. The truth is that, by definition, no one knows who the Moshiach is. The Rambam says that even his own parents and relatives will not be aware of his identity.

> However, the manner of his arrival will happen in a way that the Moshiach will be unknown before he [proclaims himself].... Yeshayahu, describing his appearance, said that his identity would be unknown even to his father, mother, family, or relatives, as it says, "He grew like a sapling [and like a root from arid ground; he had neither form nor grandeur]" (*Yeshayah* 53:2).
>
> (Rambam, Iggeres Teiman 4)

DANIEL: I'm confused. Do you mean that some guy is going to appear one day at the edge of a forest, and no one in the whole world will recognize him? Or that the Moshiach might be a well-known person right now, yet we don't realize his secret identity?

RABBI COHEN: While it's certainly possible that we won't know who he is at all, it's also possible that you yourself have already met him and shaken his hand, but didn't realize that you were speaking to the future Moshiach.

DANIEL: That's frustrating. Can't we narrow down the possibilities somewhat? Let's choose, say, the ten most righteous people in this generation and ask each one, "Are you the Moshiach?"

RABBI COHEN: Unfortunately, that won't work for two reasons. First, you are assuming that if we could gather the people we perceive as the most righteous of the generation, the Moshiach would definitely be included. I have no doubt that the people you'd choose would be righteous, but who are we to say who God considers the most fitting to be the Moshiach? The Gemara relates that Rav Yosef was once deathly ill and slipped into a coma. When he awoke, Rabbi Yehoshua, his father, asked him what he had seen while his soul was in Heaven. He answered that he had seen an upside-down world. The wealthy people, who are honored for their affluence in this world, are considered lowly in Heaven, while poor people, who are downtrodden in this world, are considered important in the Next. Rabbi Yehoshua told him that he had actually seen the World of Truth.

I know this *gemara* raises many interesting questions itself, but one point is certain: it isn't always clear to man who is held in the highest esteem Above. So even if you gather a group of righteous people together, it would not necessarily contain the Moshiach.

> Like the case of [Rav] Yosef the son of Rabbi Yehoshua who was ill and slipped into a coma. [After he regained consciousness] his father asked him, "What did you see?" He answered, "I saw an inverted world. The ones who are great [in this world] are low [in the World to Come], and the ones who are low [in

this world] are great [in the World to Come]." He replied, "You have seen a clear world."

(*Bava Basra* 10b)

"The ones who are great are low" — those who are esteemed here [in this world] because of their wealth, I saw that there [in Heaven] they are lowly. "The ones who are low are great" — I saw poor people, who are considered lowly among us, there [in Heaven] they are esteemed.

(*Rashi*, ad. loc.)

Yet there is a second, more fundamental reason why your plan won't work. You won't be able to ask someone if he is the Moshiach, because he won't know the answer. The person who is destined to be the Moshiach will not realize beforehand that he is the Moshiach.

And then, on the day of the set time...he will merit to be the re-deemer...and then he will realize himself that he is the Moshiach.

(Rabbi Chaim Vital, *Arba Mei'os Shekel Kessef*, quoted in *Otzros Acharis HaYamim*, vol. 2, ch. 6)

DANIEL: How can that be?

RABBI COHEN: It surprised me the first time I heard it, too. But if you think about it for a moment, you'll remember that we even have a precedent for this idea.

DANIEL: Oh! Moshe Rabbeinu!

RABBI COHEN: Of course. Not only did Moshe Rabbeinu not know that he was destined to be the first redeemer of the Jewish people, but he even argued the point. And who knows? Maybe the Moshiach will also humbly claim that he is not worthy of the task.

Moshe replied to God, "Please, my Master, I am not a man of words, not since yesterday nor since the day before yesterday, nor since You first spoke to Your servant, for I am heavy of mouth and heavy of speech. Then God said to him, "Who makes a mouth for man or who makes one dumb or deaf or seeing or blind? Is it not I, God? So now go! I shall be your mouth and teach you what you should say." He replied, "Please, my Master, send whomever You will send."

(Shemos 4:10–13)

Regarding the coming of the [Moshiach, the] descendant of David, I must present the following point. Moshe Rabbeinu, peace upon him, the first redeemer, lived for eighty years with no knowledge or inkling that he would redeem Israel. When the Holy One, blessed is He, told him, "I will send you to Pharaoh," Moshe even demurred, unwilling to accept the appointment. So too, God willing, will it be with the final redeemer....

And just as Shaul received the spirit of rulership and *ruach hakodesh* only after he had been anointed, while beforehand he did not recognize [his potential], the same was true of the first redeemer, and the same will be true of the last redeemer. That righteous person does not realize himself....

(Chasam Sofer, Responsa, vol. 6, 98, s.v. *"hareini nazir")*

DANIEL: If even the Moshiach himself doesn't realize his inherent potential, how are we supposed to identify him? It's hopeless.

RABBI COHEN: Not at all. As a matter of fact, this is where hope begins.

DANIEL: It is?

RABBI COHEN: Absolutely. Now that we understand that it is impossible to know for certain who the Moshiach will be, we can look calmly and rationally at what the Sages said about how we can properly identify the Moshiach.

DANIEL: I'm all ears.

RABBI COHEN: If you remember what we learned last week, you'll see that you already know the first and foremost answer to your question. Take a look at the following words of the Rambam:

"And if a king of the House of David, who is versed in Torah and occupied with mitzvos as David his ancestor, in both the Written Torah and the Oral Law, rises and influences the entire Jewish people to walk in the [Torah's] path and strengthen their observance and fights the wars of God, we can assume he is the Moshiach. And if he continues and succeeds in defeating the surrounding [enemy] nations, rebuilding the Beis HaMikdash, and gathering the exiles, he is definitely the Moshiach" (Rambam, *Hilchos Melachim* 11:4).

The Rambam is saying that the Moshiach has specific goals that he must accomplish in order to give the Jewish people the requisite peace of mind to serve God completely. He must bring the Jewish nation to Israel, end anti-Semitism, and rebuild the Beis HaMikdash, among other things. This gives us a litmus test for identifying the Moshiach. If a person arrives and accomplishes these feats, we will know for certain that he is the Moshiach.

It is also important to note the Rambam's concept of an "assumed Moshiach," a person who has accomplished some, but not all, of the tasks designated for the Moshiach. In essence, he is saying that we don't have to worry about identifying the redeemer at all. If a person matches the traits that we will discuss in a moment and begins to function as a redeemer, we assume him to be the Moshiach and will treat him as such. If he completes the tasks and turns out to be the real Moshiach, so much the better.

DANIEL: What happens if he ends up accomplishing only some of the goals? Say, he rebuilds the Beis HaMikdash but does not gather all the exiles to Eretz Yisrael. What then?

RABBI COHEN: If this person dies before accomplishing some of the designated tasks, we know retroactively that he was not Moshiach ben David. He may have been a righteous person and a God-fearing Jew, but he was not the Moshiach.

> And if he does not succeed entirely or he is killed, we realize that he was not the one promised in the Torah. Rather [we view him] as all the other perfect and kosher kings of the House of David who died.
>
> (Rambam, *Hilchos Melachim* 11:4)

DANIEL: I understand the concept, but there's still something missing. This acid test helps us to identify the Moshiach only post de facto. Are there any guidelines that can help us identify a potential Moshiach? Is there any way to verify the messianic claim of someone who has still accomplished nothing?

RABBI COHEN: Well, let's put it this way. Ultimately, as the Rambam said, there is no need to identify the Moshiach. When he accomplishes the required tasks, he will be the Moshiach, and not before then. However, there are certain characteristics we know the Moshiach will possess.[3] It's important to know these characteristics, because if a person who claims he's the Moshiach lacks some or all of them, he is instantly disqualified.

Let's start with one we have already mentioned in passing. We know that God promised King David that his progeny would rule the Jewish people forever. Therefore we know that the Moshiach must be a descendant of King David.

Your house and your kingdom will remain steadfast forever before you; your throne will remain steadfast forever.

(*Shmuel* II 7:16)

A staff will shoot from the stem of Yishai, and a branch will
grow from his roots.

(*Yeshayah* 11:1)

Included in this principle is the fact that the Jewish nation will
never have another king other than a descendant of King
Shlomo of the House of David.

(Rambam, *Peirush HaMishnayos, Sanhedrin, Chelek*)

DANIEL: Is that really possible? Is there anyone who can actually
trace his lineage back to King David these days?

RABBI COHEN: Without question. One well-known example is the
Maharal of Prague, who lived in the sixteenth century. He was able
to trace his lineage to the line of Rav Hai Gaon, who lived in the
tenth century, traditionally a descendant of King David. There are
many families that can trace their lineage to the Maharal.

Next, we know that the Moshiach will be both righteous and a
talmid chacham. He will be more wise even than King Shlomo, the
wisest man ever.

The spirit of God will rest upon him — a spirit of wisdom and
understanding, a spirit of council and strength, a spirit of
knowledge and fear of God.

(*Yeshayah* 11:2)

Righteousness will be the girdle of his loins, and faith will be
the girdle of his waist.

(*Yeshayah* 11:5)

And if a king of the House of David, who is versed in Torah and occupied with mitzvos as David his ancestor, in both the Written Torah and the Oral Law...

(Rambam, *Hilchos Melachim* 11:4)

Because the king who arises from the descendants of David will be more wise than Shlomo.

(Rambam, *Hilchos Teshuvah* 9:2)

The Moshiach will be exceedingly righteous and will cling to God. His every action and movement will be done with the intention of fulfilling his mission...to a greater degree than even Avraham Avinu.

(Abarbanel, *Yeshuos Meshicho* 3:1)

We also know that the Moshiach will be a great prophet; the level of his prophecy will be second only to Moshe Rabbeinu's. It's possible that the Moshiach will manifest his powers of prophecy only after time. However, since the Moshiach will definitely attain the level of prophecy, we know that he must possess the prerequisite qualities necessary to attain it.

Never again has a prophet like Moshe arisen in Israel.

(*Devarim* 34:10)

The Moshiach will be a great prophet, close [in stature] to Moshe Rabbeinu.

(Rambam, *Hilchos Teshuvah* 9:2)

We know that every prophet must be exceedingly wise before he receives prophecy from God because of the principle "Prophecy rests only on a person who is wise, mighty, and worthy." "Mighty" means that he has conquered his base desires. "Wealthy" refers to a person who has acquired a wealth of knowledge.

(Rambam, *Iggeres Teiman* 4)

DANIEL: But, as you said yourself about righteousness, recognizing these qualities can be highly subjective. How will we know if he is the absolutely most righteous, the most wise?

RABBI COHEN: Possibly we won't. Nevertheless, as we saw from the Rambam, an exact identification isn't crucial. As long as the person seems to possess these traits, and he begins to accomplish the designated tasks, we can assume he is the Moshiach. The final identification will not happen until he has accomplished all the goals. On the other hand, someone who is clearly not a *talmid chacham* will be instantly disqualified.

DANIEL: So much for those guys who wander the street with a sign that says, "Repent now, for I am the Messiah."

RABBI COHEN: Precisely. And there is one more unique quality the Moshiach will possess, known as *morach vada'in*, literally, he will "smell [sense] certainties." He will be able to understand the essence of a person's soul, know his spiritual record, and judge whether he is guilty or innocent.

> He will sense a person's fear of God, and he will not judge by what his eyes see or decide by what his ears hear.
>
> (*Yeshayah* 11:3)

> Rava says [the Moshiach] will be *morach vada'in*, as it says, "He will not judge by what his eyes see.... He will judge the destitute with righteousness and decide with fairness for the humble of the earth" (*Yeshayah* 11:3).
>
> (*Sanhedrin* 93b)

DANIEL: You said it's possible that the Moshiach will manifest his powers of prophecy only over time. Is the same true of *morach vada'in*?

44

RABBI COHEN: No, anyone who claims to be the Moshiach must manifest this quality from the outset. The Gemara relates that Bar Kochva, who lived during the period of the *Tannaim*, claimed that he was the Moshiach. The Sages told him that if he was really the Moshiach, he would be *morach vada'in*. When he failed their test, the Sages distanced themselves from Bar Kochva, who was eventually killed when he fell into the hands of the Romans.

If *morach vada'in* only manifests itself over time, Bar Kochva could have claimed that he hadn't developed the power yet. Therefore we can conclude that the Moshiach will possess it from the outset.[4]

> Bar Kosiva [Bar Kochva] ruled for two and a half years. He told the Rabbis, "I am the Moshiach." They replied, "It is written about the Moshiach that he will be *morach vada'in*. Let's see if you are *morach vada'in*." When they saw that he was not, they [distanced themselves from Bar Kosiva, who subsequently fell into the hands of the Romans, who] killed him.[5]
>
> (*Sanhedrin* 93b)

DANIEL: All right, let me see if I've got all this identification stuff straight. We know that from the outset the Moshiach will be an exceedingly righteous person and a great *talmid chacham*. He will be a descendant of King David and more wise even than King Shlomo. And, finally, he will have the unique attribute known as *morach vada'in*, the ability to see into another person's soul and understand his spiritual makeup. Therefore, if someone comes along who seems to possess these qualities and begins to accomplish the designated goals of the Moshiach, we assume he is the real thing. But the final identification will have to wait until he concludes those tasks, at which time we will know for certain that he is the Moshiach.

RABBI COHEN: Perfect. Just remember that at some point the Moshiach will also be a prophet of the highest order. But since it is possible that his prophecy will only develop over time, we cannot immediately disqualify a person who is lacking that aspect.

DANIEL: You know what? It seems that we have some pretty solid criteria for identifying a potential Moshiach. I suppose you were right after all.

RABBI COHEN: I'm glad to see you're finally learning something.

Week 3

In which Daniel learns the most important thing to do when you meet a missionary

DANIEL: You won't believe what happened to me yesterday.

RABBI COHEN: Actually, I probably will.

DANIEL: I was walking down a street not far from here, thinking of the questions I would ask you today, when a little old man with a long white beard fell into step beside me. He looks up at me with a big smile and says, "You look like an intelligent young man. Do you mind if I ask you a question or two about the Moshiach?"

RABBI COHEN: Uh-oh...

DANIEL: Uh-oh is right, though I didn't realize it then. At the time, I was getting ready to launch into a fascinating dissertation on the concepts we've talked about. The next thing I know, he's trying to convince me that the Moshiach has already arrived in the form of Jesus. He must have quoted a dozen verses from all over Tanach — in Hebrew, no less — to support his point.

RABBI COHEN: Let me guess. You didn't know how to refute his proofs.

DANIEL: I'm embarrassed to admit it, but, yeah. My mind went

completely blank. On an emotional level I knew he was wrong. There was something fishy about his proofs. But I couldn't put my feelings into words in order to answer him on an intellectual level.

RABBI COHEN: I'm not surprised. He's probably had years to hone his spiel to razor sharpness, and he's probably had dozens of opportunities to practice it. If the handful of verses he quoted were the sum total of your Torah knowledge, I'm sure you would also know them by heart.

DANIEL: That's not what bothered me, though. At first, I thought he had just caught me off guard...

RABBI COHEN: Which is certainly true.

DANIEL: Yes. But even after I went back to my room and thought about it for a while I realized that I still don't really know how to answer his questions. Not that I'm having a theological crisis or anything; I believe the Moshiach has yet to come. I just wish I could have refuted the missionary's claims.

RABBI COHEN: Then I suppose we have something to discuss this week. We'll talk about the specific proofs in a minute, but first I want to tell you the most important thing to do when you, or anyone who has no experience in the field, are approached by a missionary.

DANIEL: What?

RABBI COHEN: Turn around and walk the other way.

DANIEL: You're kidding, right?

RABBI COHEN: No, I'm very serious. In fact, this advice dates all the way back to the times of the Gemara. Rav Nachman said that if a person is as capable of answering a heretic as Rav Idis was, he should answer the heretic. Otherwise, he should avoid answering.

The point is, unless you are thoroughly versed in the various proofs a missionary or heretic will use and their precise refutation, as Rav Idis was, you have no business sparring with one. At best, he'll make a fool out of you, and at worst, his arguments will confuse you about basic principles of Judaism. Since you have nothing to gain, it's best that you avoid engaging in such a debate altogether.

> Rav Nachman said: One who knows how to answer a heretic [as effectively] as Rav Idis should answer; and if not, he should not answer.
>
> (*Sanhedrin* 38b)

DANIEL: So why should we bother studying the refutations?

RABBI COHEN: For three reasons. First, since we're on the subject of the Moshiach anyway, a study of these answers will bring to light many important principles about the Moshiach. Next, there are certain cases in which you have an obligation to confront a missionary. If the missionary is Jewish, for example, you must try to convince him of the truth. And if a missionary is attempting to convince Jews who lack the knowledge to defend their religion and they may fall prey to him, you must also try to counter the missionary. Finally, and most important, while it's true that you shouldn't debate a missionary unless you know what you're doing, it's important that you know these answers yourself.

DANIEL: I'll admit I'm anxious to hear what you have to say.

RABBI COHEN: Then that makes four reasons. But before we begin, I want to make one thing perfectly clear. Everything we learn here will not necessarily prepare you for the practical task of refuting a missionary. For knowledge of the most up-to-date techniques, I suggest you take one of the many classes offered by experts in the field. But don't feel you're not getting the "real deal." What we're going to learn is without question the Torah-true refutation to every false messiah who has ever appeared, Jesus included.

So let's start from the top. It's important to understand that if your first avenue of research is to deal directly with the myriad verses a missionary might use, you're heading up the wrong alley. While it's true that we could find a specific refutation for each verse, there are many more *fundamental* reasons why Jesus could not have been the Moshiach.

The first reason, and unquestionably the strongest, is one you already know.

DANIEL: I do?

RABBI COHEN: You bet. If you remember, we said that the Moshiach has certain tasks to accomplish as he helps bring the Jewish nation to perfection. We saw that the Rambam says that if a person — a potential Moshiach — begins to accomplish those tasks and seems to possess the specific, requisite character traits, we can assume that he is the Moshiach. However, the final identification will take place only after he accomplishes each and every one of those tasks.

DANIEL: I see where you're headed. Since the Beis HaMikdash has yet to be rebuilt and the Jewish nation has yet to be gathered to Eretz Yisrael, it's pretty obvious that the Moshiach has not arrived. So Jesus could not have been the Moshiach.

RABBI COHEN: Excellent. And, like I said, this is the most simple, effective method for exposing a false messiah and proving the Moshiach has still not arrived. No pretender to the title has ever passed this acid test. The Ramban made this very point more than seven hundred years ago in his famous debate with Pablo Christiani, an apostate Jew, which was presided over by King James I of Aragon.

> The Moshiach is supposed to gather the banished of Israel and the dispersed ones of Yehudah, which comprise the twelve tribes. Yeshu [Jesus], your messiah, did not gather a single person [to Eretz Yisrael].... In addition, the Moshiach is supposed to rebuild the Beis HaMikdash in Jerusalem, and Yeshu neither built nor destroyed a thing. And the Moshiach is supposed to rule every nation, but [Yeshu] did not even rule over himself. [Meaning, he could not even prevent his own execution.]
>
> (Ramban, *Sefer HaVikuach* 78)

But that's not all. There are numerous other prophecies in the Torah and *Navi* that no sane person could claim were fulfilled. The prophets state that during the time of the Moshiach the entire world will believe in God. There will no longer be strife or war, and the nations will no longer study warfare. The Moshiach will rule over the entire world. Clearly none of these prophecies have been fulfilled.

Don't limit this idea to Jesus, however. The same proof explains why Bar Kochva, Shabbsai Tzvi, and many others could not have been the Moshiach.[6]

> Referring to the Moshiach, the prophet says, "And he will dominate from sea to sea and from river to the ends of the earth" (*Tehillim* 72:8). [Yeshu, however,] was in no way a ruler. In fact, he was persecuted by his enemies, forced to hide from them, and ultimately fell into their hands. He was unable to save even himself — how could he be expected to save the entire Jewish nation?... And the prophet also says that during the time of the

51

Moshiach "they will no longer teach, each man to his friend and each man to his brother, saying, 'Know God,' for they will all know Me..." (*Yirmeyah* 31:33). And it says, "...because the earth will be as filled with knowledge of God as water covering the seabed" (*Yeshayah* 11:9). And it says, "They will beat their swords [into plowshares]...one nation will not lift a sword against another nation, and they will no longer study warfare" (ibid. 2:4). Yet from the days of Yeshu until today, the entire world has been filled with violence and robbery, and the Christians spill more blood than any other nation....

(Ramban, *Sefer HaVikuach* 49)

DANIEL: One second. This is obviously a knockout punch. How could anyone still believe that Jesus was the Moshiach?

RABBI COHEN: Very simple. They rationalized. Christian theologians invented the "second coming." In essence, they claimed that at some point Jesus will return to fulfill the designated tasks that he did not complete the first time around. But the entire concept is a clear rationalization based on the failure of Jesus to function in any way, shape, or form as the Moshiach or to fulfill any of the prophecies of the Torah and the prophets.

DANIEL: You're right. That really does seem like a pretty weak answer.

RABBI COHEN: And like the best rationalizations, they chose something that is ultimately difficult to disprove. It's impossible to prove that something will not take place in the future.

DANIEL: Like trying to prove the sun won't implode in the year 2020. We both know it's unlikely, but it would be difficult to dissuade a true believer.

RABBI COHEN: Yet anyone with a clear mind can see the truth. And as far as I'm concerned, the rest of this discussion is extraneous. Now that we've established that Jesus could not have been the Moshiach, the particulars of his life and the theological questions that a missionary might have are all irrelevant. The Ramban made this exact point during the dispute. Take a look at this quote:

"Friar Paul [Pablo Christiani] stood and asked, 'Do you believe the Messiah mentioned in the Prophets will be mortal or divine?'

"I replied, 'One moment. Originally we agreed that we would first speak of whether the Messiah has arrived, as you claim, and afterward discuss if [Yeshu] himself was divine. You still have not established that he has arrived, because I refuted all of the worthless proofs that you brought. Therefore the judgment is in my favor, because [the burden of] bringing proof is on you — you yourself accepted this [condition]. And if you do not admit that the judgment is in my favor, I agree to bring conclusive proofs, if you'll listen. After it becomes clear that this Yeshu of yours was not the Messiah, there will be no point in your arguing whether the Messiah who is destined to come to us will be mortal or what he will be.'

"The legal scholars who were present said that the judgment is in my favor on this [point]. The king told me, 'Nevertheless, answer [Friar Paul's] question' " (Ramban, *Sefer HaVikuach* 84–87).

DANIEL: Hah! Even the lawyers agreed with the Ramban.

RABBI COHEN: But even more interesting is the king's response. I like to think of it as King James syndrome: "Don't let the facts cloud the issue."

But let's continue to the next point. It's a basic principle of Judaism that in this world the Torah and mitzvos will never change. God will neither give us additional mitzvos nor cancel the ones we have already received. Jesus sought to cancel most of the mitzvos, a sure indication of an apostate. Again, this nullifies his messianic claims.

> And the ninth principle, the "cancellation." Meaning, that the Torah of Moshe will never be canceled, and there will never come another Torah from God beside it. It will never be added to or subtracted from, neither from the Written Law nor the Oral Law, as it says, "Neither add to it nor subtract from it" (*Devarim* 13:1).
>
> (Rambam, *Peirush HaMishnayos, Sanhedrin, Chelek*)

> [Yeshu] interpreted the Torah with interpretations that would lead to the cancellation of the entire Torah and all the mitzvos. Additionally, he permitted all the prohibitions of the Torah.
>
> (Rambam, *Iggeres Teiman* 1)

And there is another important point that you should keep in mind. Of all the people who have ever lived, who do you think would have made the most capable missionary of all time? Obviously Jesus himself. Yet Jesus, who was supposedly omnipotent, couldn't even manage to convince the sages of his time of his messianic claims.

DANIEL: And if Jesus himself couldn't convince the people who best understood the concept of the Moshiach, it seems pretty silly for anyone else to believe he could have been the Moshiach.

RABBI COHEN: Exactly. Again, the Ramban made this very point in the debate.

> However, I want to mention one thing that amazes me. The claims that he [Pablo Christiani] makes, telling us to believe that Yeshu was the Moshiach, are the same claims that Yeshu

himself made to our ancestors. They rejected his claims with an utter and complete refutation [despite the fact] that he [himself was speaking], who knew and could argue his opinion better than [you] the king, according to your logic that he was divine. And if our ancestors, who saw and recognized [Yeshu], did not listen to him, how can we believe and heed the voice of the king, whose only knowledge of this matter stems from distant reports, from those who heard it from people who neither knew him nor came from his lands?...

(Ramban, *Sefer HaVikuach* 103)

DANIEL: It seems like an open-and-shut case. But what about all those verses the missionary quoted? Is there any basis in the Torah or *Navi* for their claims?

RABBI COHEN: I would rather leave the specific refutations to the experts. But the truth of the matter is that I don't really see the need to refute them individually at all.

DANIEL: But didn't you say before that we would —

RABBI COHEN: Yes, I did, so pay close attention. I said that I don't feel the inclination to know or memorize the refutation to each individual verse, because they can easily be refuted in one blow.

DANIEL: Really?

RABBI COHEN: Let's put it this way. Imagine that we found a person living in the forests of Malaysia. He's never heard of the Bible and the prophets or Judaism and Christianity. Now let's suppose we give this fellow a complete set of the Tanach — the Torah, *Navi*, and *Kesuvim* — and ask him to read it from cover to cover, with only one condition. He should write down each and every clear reference that he finds of the utopian age of world peace and perfection that will take place once the Jewish nation has returned to Eretz Yisrael and the descendant of King David who will rule at that time. The list you would get would be fairly extensive, including the following verses:

" 'Behold, days are coming,' says God, 'when I will establish a righteous sprout from David; a king will reign and prosper, and he will execute justice and righteousness in the land. In his days, Judah will be safe, and Jerusalem will dwell securely' " (*Yirmeyah* 23:5).

"A staff will shoot from the stem of Yishai, and a branch will grow from his roots. And the spirit of God will rest upon him, a spirit of wisdom and understanding, a spirit of counsel and strength, a spirit of knowledge and of the fear of God.... And he will strike the [wicked of the] earth with the rod of his mouth, and with the breath of his lips he will slay the wicked. And righteousness will be the girdle of his loins and faithfulness the girdle of his waist. The wolf will dwell with the lamb, and the leopard shall lie down with the kid..." (*Yeshayah* 11:1–16).

"And it will happen in the end of days that the mountain of the Temple of God will be established as the highest of the mountains and be exalted above the hills, and all the nations will stream to it. Many peoples will go and say, 'Come, let us go up to the mountain of God, to the Temple of the God of Yaakov, and he [the Moshiach] will teach us His ways and we will walk in His paths.' For from Zion the Torah will go forth, and the Word of God from Jerusalem. He will judge between many peoples and arbitrate between distant, mighty nations. They will beat their swords into plowshares and their spears into pruning hooks. Nation will not lift up sword against nation, nor will they learn war anymore" (*Michah* 4:1–4).

And that's a very small sample. He would also record *Yirmeyah*

23:5–6, *Yeshayah* 30:7–9, *Yechezkel* 34:23–31, *Hoshea* 3:4–5, *Zechariah* 9:9–10, and many others. It's important to note that even Christian theologians agree that all of these verses are referring to the time of the Moshiach and the Moshiach himself.

The Torah expresses very clear, homogeneous ideas about the Moshiach and the world of his time. The Moshiach will be a righteous, wise, and God-fearing person who will rule the Jewish nation as a king. He will accomplish specific tasks, including rebuilding the Beis HaMikdash and the ingathering of the exiles. And the world will be a peaceful place where everyone recognizes God as the true God.

DANIEL: All this is exactly what we've been discussing these last two weeks!

RABBI COHEN: Exactly. Anyone with an objective mind will find that our idea of the Moshiach is exactly the portrait of the Moshiach that is painted by a straight reading of the Torah and *Navi*. And, as we said before, since Jesus clearly did not rebuild the Beis HaMikdash or fulfill any of the other crystal-clear prophecies, he could not have been the Moshiach.

The verses the Christians use, on the other hand, are all ambiguous and taken out of context. Our Malaysian friend would not have written down any of them, because none of them is obviously a reference to the Moshiach. Only someone with an agenda to find references would ever have thought they referred to Jesus.

DANIEL: So what the missionaries do is like shooting an arrow into a tree and then drawing a target around the arrow.

RABBI COHEN: Correct. And the funny thing is that even the Christian theologians squabble about the relative merit of many of their proofs — not surprising, considering their ambiguity. It is therefore clear that the sum value of these "proofs" is absolutely zero. The sheer number of vague references they quote means nothing. A thousand times zero —

DANIEL: Is zero. Everything you've said is logical, but there's still one thing that's bothering me. Why does God allow these guys to spread their bogus messianic claims in the first place? The Moshiach is the light at the end of the tunnel that the Jewish people have awaited for two thousand years. Why did God allow the issue to become so clouded for the vast majority of the world? Is it simply meant to be a test of our faith?

RABBI COHEN: We cannot presume to explain all of God's intentions in any matter, but I can tell you this much. There is no question that an aspect of the messiah phenomenon is meant to be a test. The Torah itself explicitly warned us of this.

> If a prophet or a dreamer of a dream should rise in your midst, and he will produce for you a sign or a wonder, and the sign or the wonder occurs of which he spoke to you saying, "Let us follow gods of others that you did not know, and we will worship them," do not listen to the words of that prophet or that dreamer of a dream, for Hashem your God is testing you to know whether you love Hashem your God with all your heart and with all your soul.
>
> (*Devarim* 13:2–6)

Yet there is an aspect of this phenomenon that goes beyond a test of faith. Imagine a world in which no one but the Jewish nation understood what the arrival of a messiah would mean. One day the Moshiach arrives and announces his presence. How do you think the world would react?

DANIEL: Well, assuming they won't know what a messiah is, they probably wouldn't know how to react at first. But eventually they would accept the truth of the Torah and the Oral Law and that the Jewish people are God's chosen nation.

RABBI COHEN: And now that the entire world knows what the Messiah represents, how do you think they will react when the Moshiach arrives?

DANIEL: After the initial shock wears off, you would probably get to the same point as before. I see your point — the second way will make a much greater impression on the world at large, because most people already have their own, different ideas about what the Moshiach will accomplish.

RABBI COHEN: Exactly. If you look back in history, you'll notice an interesting pattern. The myriad false messiahs first began to appear around the time of the destruction of the second Beis HaMikdash — never before, even during times of trouble or exile. From that point on, the world became saturated with the idea of the Messiah. True, some of their ideas run contrary to our concept of the Moshiach. But the underlying principle, the basic definition of a messiah, is known to all. Clearly God is leading the world toward our second path. When the Moshiach arrives, the contrast between His truth and the world's incorrect notions will be all the more stark.

> And all the events of Yeshu HaNotzri and [Mohammed] the Yishmaeli who arose afterward are for the sole purpose of paving the way for the Moshiach....
>
> How? The world is already filled with discussion of the Moshiach and discussion of the Torah...and when the Moshiach arises in truth...everyone will immediately return

and realize that they have inherited misinformation from their fathers....

(Rambam, *Hilchos Melachim* 11:4)

Before the time [of the redemption] each person will stray from the [correct] path.... God causes this to happen in order to publicize the concept of the Moshiach to the entire world. God fills their hearts and mouths with these concepts — even with counterfeit ideas and false ways — in order that when the time arrives...they will recognize and know that they inherited misinformation from their fathers.... If people were not concerned with [the Moshiach] before he arrived, he would not be able to verify and publicize his affairs without great difficulty upon his arrival.

(Abarbanel, *Yeshuos Meshicho* 1:1)

DANIEL: Let me sum up what we've learned. First, if a person doesn't know what he's doing, he should avoid debating a missionary. But if he must, he can make the following points: Since Jesus accomplished neither the tasks designated for the Moshiach nor the myriad prophecies, it is clear that he wasn't the Moshiach. This also refutes the claim of other pretenders such as Bar Kochva and Shabbsai Tzvi. Second, Jesus attempted to alter the laws of the Torah, which is expressly prohibited in the Torah itself. Third, if Jesus himself was refuted by the people of his time, why should we, two thousand years later, believe a missionary who's knowledge is only tenth-hand?

Regarding Christian "proofs," every verse they choose is so ambiguous that only someone with an agenda would have assumed that the verses are discussing the Moshiach in the first place. A verse that can be understood in many ways is no proof at all.

Finally, the reason God allows false messiahs to proliferate is to

60

pave the way for the Moshiach. Since the world is now highly aware of the concept and has preconceived notions regarding it, the arrival of the Moshiach as a Jewish redeemer will have all the more impact.

RABBI COHEN: Excellent! You have a lot of information to digest, so I think we'll call it a day. Next time we meet I want to get back to your questions. I assume you still have a few.

DANIEL: You bet. As a matter of fact, I already know what I want to ask. It probably should have been my very first question.

RABBI COHEN: Hmm. It doesn't take a prophet to see what's coming. Until next week.

Week 4

In which Daniel learns when the Moshiach will arrive — sort of

RABBI COHEN: Are you ready with your next question?

DANIEL: Absolutely. When exactly is the Moshiach coming?

RABBI COHEN: I was beginning to wonder when you would get around to asking that. And you might be surprised when I tell you that I can actually answer that question.

DANIEL: You can?

RABBI COHEN: Sort of.

DANIEL: Huh, I knew it.

RABBI COHEN: But before we discuss the question of when the Moshiach will arrive, let's make sure we've got a firm grasp on the concept of awaiting the Moshiach.

There are many verses that refer explicitly to a person who will arrive someday to redeem the Jewish nation from the present exile. A descendant of King David, he will ultimately rule over the Jewish people as king and teacher. Although the word *Moshiach*, which literally means "anointed one," is never actually used in Tanach in connection with this future redeemer, the Sages refer to this person as the Moshiach.

"Behold, days are coming," says God, "when I will establish a righteous sprout from David; a king will reign and prosper, and he will execute justice and righteousness in the land. In his days, Yehudah will be safe, and Jerusalem will dwell securely."

(*Yirmeyah* 23:5)

I will establish over them a single shepherd, and he will tend them — My servant David.... I will seal a covenant of peace with them and remove evil beasts from the land, and they will dwell securely in the wilderness....

(*Yechezkel* 34:23–31)

A staff will shoot from the stem of Yishai, and a branch will grow from his roots....

(*Yeshayah* 11:1–16)

According to the Rambam, belief in the coming of the Moshiach is one of the thirteen basic tenets of Judaism.[7]

Any person who does not believe in or does not await his arrival does not deny the [words of] the prophets alone, but even the Torah and Moshe Rabbeinu.

(Rambam, *Hilchos Melachim* 11:1)

There are two distinct facets to this belief. One is the obligation to believe the Moshiach will arrive. Second is the obligation to await the Moshiach and to fervently hope for his arrival.[8]

Though he may tarry, await him, for he will surely arrive; he will not delay.

(*Chavakuk* 2:3)

Rava said: When they bring a person to his [final] judgment, they ask him... "Did you await redemption?"

(*Shabbos* 31a)

The twelfth principle [deals with] the days of the Moshiach, that [a person is obligated] to believe and affirm that he will come....

(Rambam, *Peirush HaMishnayos, Sanhedrin, Chelek*)

The belief in the coming of the Moshiach is incumbent on every person who observes the Torah of Moshe.... This is because the Torah explicitly mentions the obligation to believe the words of the prophets, as it says, "[A prophet from your midst...Hashem, your God, shall establish for you;] to him shall you listen" (*Devarim* 18:15), and the prophets prophesied the coming of the Moshiach. It is clear that any person who does not believe in the coming of the Moshiach denies the words of the prophets and transgresses a positive commandment.

(*Sefer HaIkarim* 4:42)

DANIEL: Isn't it remotely possible that God will change His mind? I don't mean that literally, but what if the Jewish people have fallen so low that we no longer deserve the Moshiach and redemption? I mean, have you taken a look at the state of the Jewish nation lately?

RABBI COHEN: I could argue with your assessment of the Jewish people, but it has no bearing on the answer. Regardless of our spiritual level, God will never forsake the Jewish people.

It was taught in a *braisa*, "I will not have been revolted by them" (*Vayikra* 26:44). [This verse is referring to] the time of the Chaldeans, for I appointed Daniel, Chananiah, Mishael, and Azariah to [save] them.

"And I have not rejected them" — in the time of the Greeks, for I appointed Shimon HaTzaddik, the Chashmonai and his sons, and Mattisyahu Kohen Gadol to [save] them.

"To destroy them" — in the times of Haman, for I

appointed Mordechai and Esther to [save] them.

"To break my covenant with them" — in the time of the Persians, for I appointed the [sages] of the house of Rebbi and the sages of the various generations to [save] them.

"For Hashem is their God" — in the time to come, when no nation or people will be able to dominate them.

(Megillah 11a)

Because there is a set time for the redemption, even if Israel is completely wicked, Heaven forbid.

(Ohr HaChaim, Vayikra 25:28)

The Ramban mentions an exceedingly strong proof for this concept. If you read through the Torah, you will find mention of many punishments that the Jewish people will receive if they do not serve God — famine, drought, falling into the hands of our enemies, to name a few. However, there is not one single mention in the entire Tanach of God forsaking the Jewish people entirely or replacing them with another nation. It is clear that although they will be punished if they transgress God's commandments, God will never replace them.[9]

Nevertheless, our redemption is in our hands if we return to God. We did not lose [the potential for redemption] because of our many transgressions, and its time has not passed during our long years of rebellion. For Moshe, our master, *alav hashalom*, admonished us with many types of ultimatums and warnings, which frightened us with all manner of dread and fear about what would happen to us [if we transgress the mitzvos]. Yet God never went beyond those warnings to say that if we continue to transgress He will exchange us for another nation or forget us entirely.

(Ramban, *Sefer HaGeulah* 1)

DANIEL: I think I've got the basics. We have an obligation to await the Moshiach and to hope for his imminent arrival. We also know that God will never forsake the Jewish people. Is this where we get to discuss when the Moshiach will arrive?

RABBI COHEN: We're coming to that now. You want to know when the Moshiach will arrive. If you're asking me to give you a precise date, unfortunately I can't help you. In fact, it's impossible to calculate the exact date.

> The first thing you must know is that it is impossible for a person to ever know the definite date [of the arrival of the Moshiach], as Daniel explained and said, "Because the matters are obscured and sealed [until the time of the end]" (*Daniel* 12:9).
>
> (Rambam, *Iggeres Teiman* 3)

The fact that a person cannot know the definite date of redemption was also true of previous exiles. The Egyptian exile, for example, was known by the Jewish people to be four hundred years long. Nevertheless, because they were uncertain as to when the exile began, they did not know precisely when it was supposed to end. Even more so, it is impossible to calculate the redemption from the current exile, which will last for an unknown duration.

> Know that even when God revealed the length [of the exile], meaning the Egyptian exile, as it says, "And they will serve them and oppress them for four hundred years" (*Bereishis* 15:13), they did not know the true [date of the redemption], and the matter fell into doubt. Some people thought that [God's words] meant four hundred years from the time Yaakov descended to Egypt, and some people thought they meant four

hundred years from the beginning of servitude.

(Rambam, Iggeres Teiman 3)

Even Daniel, a prophet, reckoned the date of the redemption from the Babylonian exile incorrectly.

> Rava said: Even Daniel erred in this calculation, as it says, "In the first year of his reign I, Daniel, contemplated the calculation" (*Daniel* 9:2). Since he said, "I contemplated," we can infer that he [originally] erred.

(Megillah 12a)

DANIEL: But doesn't it say in the end of *sefer Daniel* that an angel revealed the date of the Moshiach's arrival to him? Granted, the answer was in code, but couldn't we puzzle out the meaning if we examine the angel's words carefully enough?

RABBI COHEN: It's certainly true that the prophecy you're referring to contains the date.

> Rabbi Yirmeyah said, and some say Rabbi Chiya bar Abba said: The *Targum* [translation] of the Torah was composed by Onkelus HaGer [who learned it] from Rabbi Eliezer and Rabbi Yehoshua. The *Targum* of the Prophets was composed by Yonasan ben Uziel, [who learned it] from Chaggai, Zechariah, and Malachi. Eretz Yisrael shook over an area of four hundred *parsah* by four hundred *parsah* [when the *Targum* of the Prophets was composed]. A Heavenly voice called out, saying, "Who is this who has revealed My secrets to mortal beings?" Yonasan ben Uziel rose to his feet and said, "I am the one who revealed Your secrets to mortal beings. It is revealed and known to You that I did not act for my own glory or for the glory of my father's house, but rather for Your glory, that disagreement should not spread in Israel." Yonasan ben Uziel also

wished to reveal the *Targum* of Writings. A Heavenly voice called out and said to him, "Enough!" Why [was he not granted permission to compose the *Targum* of Writings]? Because [Writings] contains the date of [the arrival of] the Moshiach.

(*Megillah* 3a)

In fact, it's probable that there are many references to the date hidden in the words of the Torah and Prophets. But there are two major problems with attempting any calculations. The first problem is that the Sages explicitly prohibited such an attempt.[10]

DANIEL: But why?

RABBI COHEN: Imagine that a great, modern-day rabbi predicted that the Moshiach would arrive exactly ten years into the future. Every Jewish person heard and accepted the prediction. But for some reason, the date passes with nary a messianic stir. What do you suppose would happen?

DANIEL: Nothing good, I guess. The more they believed, the worse it would be.

RABBI COHEN: At the very least, there would be great disappointment and depression. Worse, people would lose faith in God and the coming of the Moshiach. The *Rishonim* relate many incidents virtually identical to my example. In extreme cases, the Jews even went so far as to threaten their gentile neighbors with Heavenly retribution for past faults or to sell their land for pennies on the dollar, assuming the land would be worthless once the Moshiach arrived and they left for Eretz Yisrael. Unfortunately, when the Moshiach failed to appear, it was their gentile neighbors who sought retribution.

Rav Shmuel bar Nachmani said in the name of Rabbi Yonasan:

May the bones of those who calculate dates [of the end of the exile] suffer agony! For [people] say, "Since the date has arrived and [the Moshiach] did not come, he will never come."

(*Sanhedrin* 87b)

For this reason Chazal warned against calculating dates or appointing times for the coming of the Moshiach, because it will cause the public to stumble and cause doubt to enter their hearts when the time arrives and the Moshiach does not arrive. This [is what they meant when] they said, "May the bones of those who calculate dates [of the end of the exile] suffer agony!" — because they are a stumbling block for people.

(Rambam, *Iggeres Teiman* 3)

There is a second, more subtle reason the Sages prohibited calculating the date. As we said before, we are obligated to fervently hope for the arrival of the Moshiach. Now let's suppose you manage to decipher the conversation between Daniel and the angel and figure out that, beyond a doubt, the Moshiach will arrive in exactly ten years. For the next ten years, you would have a difficult time, to say the least, believing that the Moshiach might arrive at any moment. Therefore, the Sages prohibited the calculations in the first place.

Also, if he specifies a time, he will not believe that [the Moshiach might] arrive before that time....

(Mabit, *Beis Elokim, Sha'ar HaYesodos* 50)

Besides the prohibition of the Sages, there is a second problem inherent in attempting to calculate the date. Simply, God desires that the date remain hidden.

However, I think their mistake was [caused by] the will of God to conceal the date [of the arrival of the Moshiach], as Daniel said, "Let many muse and let knowledge increase" (*Daniel* 12:4), and not because the date is intrinsically hidden in that book.

(Ramban, Sefer HaGeulah 4)

DANIEL: Hmmm...that would tend to thwart any attempts. It also explains why the Rambam said it is impossible to calculate the date and the historical difficulty that the Jewish people have had in their calculations. But it still doesn't explain why God conceals the date. Why does God mind if I figure out when the Moshiach will arrive?

RABBI COHEN: As we've already said, we can never presume to explain all of God's intentions in any matter. Yet this is what we know: It is an intrinsic facet of an exile that its exact ending be unknown. If a person knew exactly when the redemption would come, it would greatly mitigate the burden of the exile. He would think, *Sure, life is difficult now, but on such-and-such date I'll be free.* If not him, his children or even grandchildren would go free. Exile is such a painful state precisely because of its uncertainty. God has clearly decided that, for the time being, we still belong in exile.

Because when the date is revealed, there is already, in essence, a redemption, for if someone knows the time he will leave, it is as if he is already redeemed.

(Maharal, Netzach Yisrael 24)

Alternatively, if a person really did know that the redemption would occur only in the very distant future — even hundreds of years — he might lose faith entirely.

It was hidden to them, lest it be a stumbling block if it became known to successive generations and they despaired of the exile if [the date of the arrival of the Moshiach] were very distant.

(*Yefeh To'ar, Midrash Rabbah, Bereishis* 98:2,
s.v. *"l'galos lahem hakeitz"*)

DANIEL: Now I'm confused. First you answer that you can "sort of" tell me when the Moshiach will arrive, and now you prove that it's impossible to even know.

RABBI COHEN: I can't tell you the date when the Moshiach will arrive, but I can tell you the underlying principles that govern the time of his arrival. There are two possible times for the arrival of the Moshiach. First, the Moshiach will come when the Jewish nation does *teshuvah* voluntarily. Second, there is a set time when the redemption will arrive regardless of our actions. As soon as either event occurs, the Moshiach will come immediately.[11]

Rabbi Alexandri said: Rabbi Yehoshua ben Levi noted a contradiction. It says "in its time" (*Yeshayah* 60:20), but it also says, "I will hasten it" (ibid.). [The answer is that] if [the Jewish people] deserve, "I will hasten it." If they do not deserve, "[I will bring the redemption] in its time."

(*Sanhedrin* 98a)

Rabbi Yochanan said: God, blessed is He, said to Israel, "Even though I set a limit to the date when [the Moshiach] will arrive, whether or not you do *teshuvah* he will arrive at the appointed time. Nevertheless, if you do *teshuvah* for even one day, I will bring him before the appointed time.

(*Shemos Rabbah* 25:16)

Therefore, God should have mercy, we believe that He set two times for [the end of] our servitude [exile]. One is the time [when the Moshiach will arrive if we do] *teshuvah*, and the second is the final time. Whichever occurs first will make us fitting for redemption; if we do *teshuvah*, [God] will [bring the Moshiach immediately and] not pay attention to the final time.... And if we do not do *teshuvah*, we will remain [in exile] until the final time.

(Rav Sa'adyah Gaon, Emunos V'Deos 8:2)

In essence, there are two "paths" to the Moshiach, one through voluntary *teshuvah* and one through reaching the final date that God has established for the redemption. However, the redemption will differ according to the path we choose. If the Jewish nation repents voluntarily, the redemption will be a miraculous, wondrous event. If not, the redemption will be an extended and mundane process that will appear to be a "natural," unfolding of historical events. This fundamental principle is vital for understanding many verses in Tanach and statements of the Sages concerning the Moshiach. Take a look, for example, at the following verses:

"I was watching in night visions and, behold, with the clouds of Heaven, one like a man came" (*Daniel* 7:13).

"Behold, your king will come to you; righteous and victorious is he, a humble man riding on a donkey..." (*Zechariah* 9:9).

On the surface, the two verses contradict one another. The verse in *Daniel* speaks of the Moshiach's appearance in glowing terms, as a wonderful, miraculous spectacle. The verse in *Zechariah*, on the other hand, speaks of his arrival as a mundane event. Using our principle, the question is answered. If the Jewish people do *teshuvah* voluntarily and bring the Moshiach themselves, the arrival of the Moshiach will be miraculous. If not, the Moshiach will come at the appointed time, but in a mundane manner.

Rabbi Alexandri said: Rabbi Yehoshua ben Levi noted a

contradiction. It says, "Behold, with the clouds of Heaven, one like a man came" (*Daniel* 7:13), but it also says "a humble man riding on a donkey" (*Zechariah* 9:9). [The answer is that] if [the Jewish people] deserve, "with the clouds of Heaven." If they do not deserve, "a humble man, riding on a donkey."

(*Sanhedrin* 98a)

The repetition of the subject and the variation in language is explained by the words of Chazal, who said that if the redemption will occur by means of the merit of Israel, it will be a marvelous event, and the redeemer will be revealed from the heavens with wonders and miracles. On the other hand, if the redemption occurs on the final date, and Israel is not deserving, it will occur in another manner. On this [situation] it is said that the redeemer will come as "a humble man riding on a donkey" (*Zechariah* 9:9).

(*Ohr HaChaim, Bemidbar* 24:17, s.v. "*v'keifel ha'inyan*")

Using this idea, we can also finally give the second answer to a question we dealt with the first week. If you recall, we found what seemed to be a contradiction between two *midrashim*. One *midrash* states clearly that the Moshiach will rebuild the Beis HaMikdash, while another claims the future Beis HaMikdash will drop from Heaven, fully built.

DANIEL: Wait — I see it. If the Jewish nation does *teshuvah* voluntarily, the Beis HaMikdash will fall from Heaven. But if not, the Moshiach will arrive at the set time and rebuild the Beis HaMikdash himself.

The [normal] order of events is that the Beis HaMikdash will be rebuilt by man. Nevertheless, there is a possibility that the Beis HaMikdash will hasten to descend before it is built below.

(*VaYoel Moshe, Ma'amar Shalosh Shavuos* 61)

RABBI COHEN: Exactly. As we continue to study the principles of the Moshiach and his era, we will see more ramifications of this idea, but for now, we have an answer to your question of when the Moshiach will arrive. He will arrive when the Jewish people do *teshuvah* voluntarily or when the date chosen by God arrives.

DANIEL: Since we're already on the subject, I have one last question. You said that if the Jewish people do *teshuvah* voluntarily the Moshiach will come immediately. So clearly, every bit of personal *teshuvah* will help to bring the Moshiach sooner. Are there any other specific things the Sages mention that help to bring the Moshiach?

RABBI COHEN: Absolutely. Although Torah and *tefillah* are important to the Jewish people for many reasons, the Sages mention them specifically in connection with the redemption. Both have the power to hasten the arrival of the Moshiach.

> When Israel cries before Him, the redemption will come....
>
> (*Midrash Rabbah, Shemos* 32:9)

> "Their outcry, because of the work, went up to God" (*Shemos* 2:23) — because even though the time had arrived, they were not deserving of redemption. Rather, since they cried profusely to God due to the servitude, [He] accepted their prayers...to hint that the coming of the redemption depends on *teshuvah* and prayer.
>
> (Rabbeinu Bachyai, *Shemos* 2:23)

> Ulla said: This verse is stated in the Aramaic language: "If all [the Jews] study Torah, I will gather them now."
>
> (*Bava Basra* 8a)

> Rabbi Alexandri said: Whoever engages in Torah for its own sake promotes peace among the Heavenly host and among the earthly

host.... And Levi said: He even hastens the redemption....

(*Sanhedrin* 99b)

DANIEL: All right, let me sum up what we've learned. Belief in the coming of the Moshiach is one of the thirteen basic tenets of faith. This belief is actually comprised of two parts, the obligation to believe the Moshiach will arrive and the obligation to hope for his imminent arrival. We know that regardless of the spiritual state of the Jewish people, God will never forsake them and will redeem them anyway.

We said that it's impossible to calculate the exact date of the redemption because God desires that the date remain hidden. The Sages also prohibited such calculations because of the dangers involved in a wrong guess. However, we do know that there are two possible times when the Moshiach might arrive. If the Jewish people do *teshuvah* voluntarily, the Moshiach will arrive immediately. Otherwise, there is a final, set time when the Moshiach will arrive.

Finally, we mentioned that there are certain things we can do that earn us the merit of bringing a speedy redemption, such as prayer, *teshuvah*, and Torah study.

But...well, it's still not clear.

RABBI COHEN: What?

DANIEL: Well, we've learned the theory that governs the arrival of the Moshiach, and I admit that helps me to understand the concept. But somehow it seems I'm back where I started. No one can say when the Jewish people will finally get in gear and do *teshuvah*, and the final date is hidden, so I still have no idea when the Moshiach will arrive. Isn't there anything else you can tell me about when to expect him?

RABBI COHEN: As a matter of fact, if we tackle the subject from a different angle, there is quite a bit more to discuss. But I think it should wait until next week. We've covered enough material for one session.

DANIEL: Sigh... Forever in suspense.

RABBI COHEN: I try, I try. Until next week.

Week 5

In which Daniel learns what the world will be like before the Moshiach arrives and how the Sages figured it all out

RABBI COHEN: Are you ready?

DANIEL: Sure am.

RABBI COHEN: Great. I said last week that if we want to know when the Moshiach will arrive, we still have a second avenue for investigation. Throughout the Gemara and Midrash are many descriptions of the state of the world during the time the Moshiach arrives. So all we need to do is examine these descriptions of the era of the Moshiach and see if they match the present world.

DANIEL: If they match, we must be living in the era of the Moshiach, and if not, we wait until we see the signs. That sounds easy enough.

RABBI COHEN: The first thing you need to know is that the generation immediately preceding the arrival of the Moshiach will be characterized by rampant troubles for the Jewish people and ignorance of God. The Sages referred to this period as *"chevlei Moshiach,"* literally, "the birth pangs of the Moshiach." Just as a mother experiences intense pain when bringing a child into this world, the redeemer's arrival will be preceded by a period of trials and tribulations. In fact, some of the Sages professed a desire that they not witness the coming of the Moshiach, fearing the conditions of that generation.

Like a pregnant woman close to giving birth, she is in pain; she screams in her pangs. So were we before You, God.

(*Yeshayah* 26:17)

We see renewed afflictions and conclude that they are signs of salvation and redemption, for we have been promised that we will be redeemed amid trouble and afflictions, like a woman in labor.

(*Rashi*, ad. loc.)

"There will be a time of trouble such as there has never been since there was a nation until that time. And at that time your nation will escape" (*Daniel* 12:1) — these are the birth pangs of the Moshiach, meaning pain and suffering. And just as a woman in childbirth no longer experiences difficulty after the birth, for her spirit is immediately revived and she [once again] believes in life, so too will Israel be at that time. They will have immediate relief from the hands of their enemies, for [Moshiach] the king will be revealed, and "sadness and sighing will flee."

(*Midrash Daniel* 12:11, quoted in
Chevlei Moshiach BiZemaneinu, p. 86)

Ulla said: May [the Moshiach] come, but may I not see him. And so said Rabbah: May [the Moshiach] come, but may I not see him.

(*Sanhedrin* 98b)

DANIEL: So we're doomed?

RABBI COHEN: Not exactly. There are two points you need to keep in mind. First, the Sages specifically addressed your concern and answered that there is, in fact, a way to guard oneself from the birth pangs of the Moshiach. They said that to avoid the troubles that will befall the world and the Jewish people during the era preceding the arrival of the Moshiach, a person should concentrate on learning Torah and performing acts of *chesed*. The Maharal explains that Torah is the ultimate good in the spiritual realm, while *chesed* is the ultimate good in the physical realm. A person who excels in both aspects will be completely shielded from the "evil" of the birth pangs of the Moshiach, travails of both physical and spiritual nature.

> Rabbi Elazar was asked by his students, "What can a person do to be spared from the birth pangs of the Moshiach?" [He answered,] "One should occupy oneself with Torah and acts of *chesed.*"
>
> (*Sanhedrin* 98b; see also Maharal, ad. loc., s.v. *"v'ka'amar lei"*)

It is also possible that the Jewish nation will avoid the birth pangs of the Moshiach entirely. Do you remember the concept of "two paths to the Moshiach" that we discussed last week?

DANIEL: Sure. Basically there are two possibilities for the arrival of the Moshiach — either through the voluntary *teshuvah* of the Jewish people or when we reach the date that God set for the redemption.

RABBI COHEN: Right. And the specifics of the redemption may vary according to the way in which the Moshiach arrives. The concept of the birth pangs of the Moshiach is a further example of how the redemption might differ. According to Rav Sa'adyah Gaon and other *Rishonim*, the birth pangs will occur only if the Jewish nation fails to repent voluntarily.

> I will discuss the two situations together. Meaning, if we do not return [to God in repentance], the events of Moshiach ben Yosef [and the era preceding his arrival will] occur. And if we do *teshuvah* and exempt ourselves from these events, Moshiach ben David will immediately be revealed....
>
> (Rav Sa'adyah Gaon, *Emunos V'Deos* 8:6)

> This means to say, if the time of the redemption arrives and "wine" is not found, meaning, we are lacking in Torah, the redemption will occur by means of a burdensome and powerful exile, during which the nations will oppress Israel....
>
> (*Ohr HaChaim, Bereishis* 49:11, s.v. "*u'bedam anavim*")

DANIEL: What kind of troubles are we talking about?

RABBI COHEN: Let's start with the world at large. The Sages say that the generation that precedes the arrival of the Moshiach will be characterized by insolence, a lack interpersonal respect, and the corruption of its most honored citizens. Young people will insult their elders, yet elders will honor the young. People will no longer feel shame for even the most immoral behavior. The world will no longer believe in God, and the religious will be ridiculed as anachronistic and foolish.

> Rabbi Nehorai says: In the generation when the son of David will come, young people will shame the elderly, and the elderly will rise before young people. A daughter will stand against her mother, and a daughter-in-law [will stand] against her mother-in-law. The face of the generation will be like the face of a dog, and a son will not be embarrassed before his father.
>
> (*Sanhedrin* 97a)

Rabbi Nechemiah says: In the generation when the son of David will come, insolence will increase and honor will be corrupted [diminish]. The vine will produce its fruit, yet wine will be expensive. The entire kingdom will convert to heresy, and there will be no rebuke.

(Sanhedrin 97a)

They will not respect one another. Another version: "Honor will be corrupted" — their honored ones will be warped and corrupt.

(Rashi, ad. loc.)

"There will be no rebuke" — no person will be capable of giving rebuke, because they will all commit transgressions, and when they rebuke [another person], they will answer, "You [transgress] as I do."

(Rashi, Sotah 49b, s.v. "v'ein tochachah")

What [is the meaning of the verse] "Truth will be absent, and turning from evil will become foolish" (Yeshayah 59:15)? In the academy of Rabbi Sheila they said: Whoever turns away from evil will be considered foolish by the people.

(Sanhedrin 97a)

The Jewish nation will also undergo many changes before the arrival of the Moshiach. The number of Torah scholars and students will decrease. A large portion of the Jewish people will leave the fold of Judaism, and those who remain true to the faith will be dubbed foolish. The nation as a whole will be plagued by troubles of all kinds.

What enters your minds will not be. As for what you say, "We will be like the [other] nations, like the families of the land, to worship wood and stone."

(Yechezkel 20:32)

Rabbi Yochanan said: In the generation when the son of David will come, [the number of] Torah scholars will decrease, and the rest [of the people], their eyes will become worn out with grief and worry. Numerous troubles will constantly appear; before the first [trouble] is over, a second will quickly appear.

(*Sanhedrin* 97a)

The master Daniel explained to us what God informed him: that when the exile lengthens and the troubles afflict us continually, many will become disconnected from the [Jewish] religion. Doubt will enter their hearts, and they will go astray because of their perception of our weakness and the might of those who rise against us and their power over us. [Nevertheless,] a small portion of people will neither doubt nor lose their faith, [as Daniel] said, "They will be clarified and cleansed and refined by many; and the wicked will act wickedly, and none of the wicked will understand, and the wise will understand" (*Daniel* 12:10).

(Rambam, *Iggeres Teiman* 1)

DANIEL: One second. Are you saying that *this* is the generation of the Moshiach? Your description sure seems to match our own.[12]

RABBI COHEN: I'm not saying anything — the Sages are. But I certainly agree that our generation bears a remarkable resemblance to the one I've described. I'm not surprised. Seventy years ago the Chafetz Chaim declared that we are living in the period known as *ikvesa d'Meshicha*, the "footsteps of the Moshiach," a time when he is so close that we can almost hear him approaching.

DANIEL: Does that mean the Moshiach will definitely arrive within the next few years?

RABBI COHEN: I certainly hope so, though not necessarily. In essence, we've described the generation in which the Moshiach will arrive. If that description matches the world around us, so much the better. It should strengthen our hope in the imminent arrival of the Moshiach and serve as an impetus to bring us closer to God. Our world, however, might match the Sages' descriptions for a long time to come, so we can never be sure.

DANIEL: But why is it that the Jewish people have to go through the birth pangs of the Moshiach before he arrives? You've explained the nature of the footsteps of the Moshiach, but you haven't explained why we have to experience all these troubles. Can't he arrive in peace?

RABBI COHEN: It is clear that the Moshiach will arrive after a period of pain and tribulation, so your question is astute. Why?

To understand the answer, remember the link we established between *teshuvah* and redemption (week 4). As soon as the Jewish nation does *teshuvah*, the Moshiach will arrive. The birth pangs of the Moshiach will act as a catalyst for the Jewish people to do *teshuvah*. Obviously the greater the suffering, the greater the impetus to do *teshuvah*.[13]

> When you are in distress and all these things have befallen you at the end of days, you will return to Hashem your God and listen to His voice.
>
> (*Devarim* 4:30)

> Rabbi Yudah says: If Israel does not do *teshuvah*, they will not be redeemed — and Israel will do *teshuvah* only amid suffering, amid wandering, and because they lack sustenance.
>
> (*Pirkei D'Rabbi Eliezer* 3, quoted in *Chevlei Moshiach BiZemaneinu*, p. 183)

"When you are in distress" — this verse is referring to the promise of redemption. When the Jewish people are in distress, which is the time of exile...referring to the birth pangs of the Moshiach...God promises that He will arouse their hearts to return in repentance. This is the meaning of "You will return to God." The verse [continues and] provides a reason for this promise: "For Hashem your God is a merciful God; He will not forsake you."

(Ohr HaChaim, Devarim 4:30)

Take a look at the following *midrash*:

" 'He sent the dove...and the dove did not find rest....' Yehudah bar Nachman said in the name of Rabbi Shimon, 'Had she found rest, she would not have returned.' Similarly it says, 'She dwelled among the nations [but] found no rest' (*Eichah* 1:3) — had she found rest, she would not have returned. Similarly it says, 'Among those nations you will not be tranquil; there will be no rest for the sole of your foot' (*Devarim* 28:65) — had they found rest, they would not have returned" (*Midrash Rabbah, Bereishis* 33:6).

The idea behind this *midrash* is the second answer to your question. If the Jewish people become too enmeshed in gentile society while in exile, they will be reluctant to return to Eretz Yisrael.[14]

To assure that the Jewish people will return to Eretz Yisrael during the redemption, God will prepare the Jewish nation by uprooting them from their comfortable existence. This preparation will take the form of the birth pangs of the Moshiach.

The manner of the ingathering is hinted at in the words "and with outpoured anger." Meaning, in the final days God will arouse the hearts of those Jews who were compelled to become apostates. They, or their descendants, will return to God and secretly observe a few mitzvos.... The hearts of the gentiles will then be aroused to persecute and plot against them for this [and they will say], "You are becoming Jewish and not conforming to gentile law!" They will burn [and murder] them cruelly by the hundreds and thousands....

Therefore the hearts of the "compelled ones," along with their children, wives, and infants, will be aroused to flee for their lives. They will flee the lands where they lived among the gentiles to escape to distant lands.

(Abarbanel, *Yechezkel* 20:34)

DANIEL: All right, one last question, but it's a tough one. How did the Sages know all this? How did they know exactly what the generation of the Moshiach would look like? Did they see the future with *ruach hakodesh*?

RABBI COHEN: It's certainly true that the *Tannaim* and *Amoraim* perceived the future with *ruach hakodesh*, but in this instance the Abarbanel provides a second explanation. He begins with the simple idea that everything is best experienced from a strong state of contrast. The light of a single candle, for example, is nearly invisible in a lighted room, yet place that same candle in a dark room and it becomes the focus of our sight. A colorful picture stands out when placed against a white background, but seems to fade when the background itself is colorful.

The Sages understood that as part of the ultimate plan for creation, God desires that the redemption and the arrival of the Moshiach also be experienced in this matter. With this idea in mind, the Sages analyzed the verses that describe the time of the Moshiach. However the verses describe the time of the Moshiach, they knew the opposite would be true of the generation preceding his arrival — the greatest contrast possible. Therefore, since the time of the Moshiach will be a wondrous time of knowledge, spirituality, and goodness, the Sages understood that the generation preceding his arrival would be characterized by hedonism, rampant troubles, and ignorance of God. A truly remarkable idea.[15]

> Chazal affirmed and accepted that when the time of salvation approaches there will be an increase in the enormous troubles that befall Israel in order to shift their affairs from extreme evil, loss, and ruin to greatness and untold success.
>
> Chazal evaluated the prophecies of the future, the types of goodness and success that the prophets designated for the days of the Moshiach, the opposite of which must precede the time of the redemption. For if the time of the redemption will be filled with knowledge of God, and everyone will know him "from their smallest to their greatest," then at the end of the exile it will be the opposite. Therefore Rabbi Yochanan said, "In the generation when the son of David will come [the number of] Torah scholars will decrease" (*Sanhedrin* 97a).[16]
>
> (Abarbanel, *Yeshuos Meshicho* 1:5)

DANIEL: Let me try to sum up what we've learned. Before the Moshiach arrives, the world will go through a stage known as *chevlei Moshiach*, a time of trials and tribulation. People will become insolent, rude, and corrupt. They'll engage in every type of immoral behavior without shame. The Jewish nation will also be affected by the times. Many Jews will become assimilated, and those who remain religious will be called foolish.

These birth pangs will shake the Jewish people from their comfortable life in exile and act as a catalyst for them to do *teshuvah*. But if the Jewish people do *teshuvah* voluntarily, it is possible for them to evade the birth pangs entirely.

Finally, the Sages understood that since every event is experienced best from a point of contrast, the arrival of the Moshiach will also happen in this way. Therefore, the nature of the world before the Moshiach arrives will be the opposite of the state of the world at the time of the Moshiach. And since during the era of the Moshiach the world will be filled with goodness and spirituality, the generation before he arrives will be a time of hedonism and afflictions.

RABBI COHEN: Excellent. Just don't forget the advice we mentioned. The more you learn Torah and do acts of *chesed*, and the more you do *teshuvah*, the more resistance you will have against the troubles of the time. Ultimately, that is the most important thing to gain from learning about the era of the Moshiach. If study of these principles serves to increase our faith and strengthen our service of God, it will make our learning sessions so much more worthwhile.

So have we answered all your questions?

DANIEL: Nope, I still have a bunch left.

RABBI COHEN: Then we'll take it from here next week.

Week 6

In which Daniel learns about the era of the Moshiach

RABBI COHEN: So what's your next question about the Moshiach?

DANIEL: There's still one area we haven't touched at all. You've told me about the Moshiach and the generation in which he'll arrive, but what will the world be like after he gets here?[17]

RABBI COHEN: A good question. Let's start from the very beginning. The Sages tell us that when the world was first created it was nearly perfect, containing only as much evil, or imperfection, required to give man free will. When Adam ate from the Tree of Knowledge, he caused a great, destructive change to take place. Both man and his surroundings were transformed in many ways. The exact nature of those changes are beyond our discussion, but suffice it to say that he caused a tremendous increase of evil in the world. It became difficult for man to overcome his desires and become close to God.

The Ramban and the Maharal both explain that during the era of the Moshiach the entire creation will return to the state of perfection that would have existed had Adam not transgressed. The intrinsic laws of nature will remain unchanged. Gravity will still cause objects to fall to the ground rather than float. People will still feel hungry and require sustenance to survive. Cars, computers, weapons, and all forms of technology will still exist in the world. Yet, at the same time, our lives will be radically altered.

> When the commandments are being fulfilled, Eretz Yisrael will be as the world was originally, before the transgression of Adam HaRishon.... Therefore, the verse states about the days of the Redeemer, who will descend from the line of Yishai, that peace will return to the world, and the preying and malignancy of wild beasts and insects will cease, as was their nature originally.
>
> (Ramban, *Vayikra* 26:6; see also Ramban, *Sefer HaVikuach* 39)

According to the opinion that states, "There is no difference between this world and the days of the Moshiach except the oppression [of Israel] by the nations," the world will behave according to its nature and custom in matters of nature. It will not behave contrary to nature, but rather it will behave in ways that are possible in nature. However, [the world will differ from now in that] everyone will be righteous....

In the future, when transgression leaves man, the ground, which God cursed because of the transgression of Adam, will return to its original state and its [inherent] blessedness, as it was before Adam transgressed. And according to the opinion that states, "There is no difference between this world and the days of the Moshiach except the oppression [of Israel] by the nations," do not find difficult what is stated here that the ground will produce fruit every day. This is not considered a miracle, because this existed at the beginning of the creation of the world [and would have remained so] had there not been transgression.

(Maharal, *Netzach Yisrael* 50)

As I've said before, now that we understand the underlying principle, that the world will return to a state of perfection, the specific details will fall into place. First and foremost, during the time of the Moshiach, every nation will believe in God. The world will also accept the Torah as God's true teaching.

> "It will be that at every New Moon and on every Sabbath all mankind will come to prostrate themselves before Me," says God.
>
> (*Yeshayah* 66:23)

> They will no longer teach — each man his friend, each man his brother — saying, "Know God." For all of them will know Me, from their smallest to their greatest.
>
> (*Yirmeyah* 31:33)

> God will be King over all the land; on that day God will be One and His Name One.
>
> (*Zechariah* 14:9)

> Everyone will return to the true faith.
>
> (Rambam, *Hilchos Melachim* 12:1)

> The only occupation of the entire world will be to know God.
>
> (Rambam, *Hilchos Melachim* 12:5)

Another major change that will take place during the time of the Moshiach is that the power of the evil inclination will be greatly reduced. A person will desire only to do good.[18]

> I will give you a new heart and put a new spirit within you; I will remove the heart of stone from your flesh and give you a heart of flesh.
>
> (*Yechezkel* 36:26)

> Since the time of the Creation, man was permitted to do as he desired...but in the days of the Moshiach, choosing good

will be natural for him.

(*Ramban, Devarim* 30:6)

Good will increase in every form, and evil will be abolished entirely. [This will affect man] both spiritually and physically, which is [what the prophet meant by the] "heart of stone" that will be transformed into a "heart of flesh." Meaning, the inclination toward good will increase in man to the extent that he will not be drawn by physical [desires] at all. Rather, he will continually lean toward serving God and following the Torah....

(Ramchal, *Ma'amar HaIkarim, "BaGeulah"*;
see also Maharal, *Netzach Yisrael* 46)

Prophecy will also return to the world during the time of the Moshiach. In our current state, prophecy is unattainable, even by a person on the proper spiritual level. The Sages relate that there were people who intrinsically deserved to receive prophecy, but did not receive it because their generation was not worthy. During the time of the Moshiach, it will become easy to attain the spiritual heights necessary for prophecy.

I will place My words in your mouth....

(*Yeshayah* 51:16)

It will happen after this, that I will pour My spirit upon all flesh, and your sons and daughters will prophesy; your elders will dream dreams, and your young men will see visions.

(*Yoel* 3:1)

Ruach hakodesh will be "poured onto all flesh and blood" to the extent that everyone will attain it without difficulty. This is what the prophet meant by, "I will pour My spirit upon all flesh" (*Yoel* 3:1).

(Ramchal, *Ma'amar HaIkarim, "BaGeulah"*)

DANIEL: If the entire creation will be perfect, I suppose that also means there will finally be world peace.

RABBI COHEN: Without question. Not only will the nations finally stop persecuting the Jewish people, but they will even make peace among themselves. This is just one example of our principle that nature will remain unchanged, yet our lives will be radically altered. Tools of war and destruction will still be around during the era of the Moshiach, yet war will cease to exist. This is the idea of the well-known verse that describes men beating their swords into plowshares. Since we won't have any need for our swords as weapons, we'll find other uses for them. Who knows? Maybe we'll find a use for the nuclear missiles stockpiled around the world today.

> They will beat their swords into plowshares and their spears into pruning hooks; nations will not lift sword against one another, and they will no longer study warfare.
>
> *(Yeshayah 2:4)*

> At that time, there will be neither hunger nor war nor jealousy and strife, for [the world] will be greatly influenced by good, and every delicacy will be as common as dust.
>
> (Rambam, *Hilchos Melachim* 12:5)

Another example of the changes that will take place is the prosperity that will spread across the globe and in Eretz Yisrael in particular.

> I will make them and the surroundings of My hill into a blessing, and I will cause the rain to fall in its time; they will be rains of blessing. The tree of the field will yield its fruit, and the earth will yield its produce....
>
> *(Yechezkel 34:26–27)*

Then you will see and be radiant, your heart will be startled and broadened, for the affluence of the West will be turned over to you, and the wealth of nations will come to you.

(*Yeshayah* 60:5 until the end of ch. 61)

"And all of your borders will [be filled with] precious gems." Rabbi Binyamin Levi said: In the future, the borders of Jerusalem will be filled with precious gems and pearls, and all of Israel will come and take what they need. For in this world Israel constructs walls using stones and pebbles, but in the World to Come they will construct walls using precious gems and pearls.

(*Yalkut Shimoni, Yeshayah* 478)

In [the Moshiach's] days people will remain stronger or weaker relative to others. [The difference is] that during those days earning a livelihood will become easier to the extent that if a person does a small amount of work, he will attain great results. This is the meaning of [the Sages'] statement, "In the future, Eretz Yisrael will bring forth bread rolls and fine woolen clothes" (*Shabbos* 30b).

(Rambam, *Peirush HaMishnayos, Sanhedrin, Chelek*)

DANIEL: But if the world really will be perfect, and we won't even need to work much to make a living, what will we do all day?

RABBI COHEN: The primary occupation of the world will be to know and understand God and His teachings. In essence, the entire world will be occupied with learning Torah.

They will no longer teach — each man his friend, each man his brother — saying, "Know God." For all of them will know Me, from their smallest to their greatest.

(*Yirmeyah* 31:33)

The only occupation of the entire world will be to know God.

(Rambam, *Hilchos Melachim* 12:5)

DANIEL: Even the gentiles? I mean, will there even be gentiles after the Moshiach arrives?

RABBI COHEN: Of course. We mentioned once (week 1) that the Moshiach will destroy the enemies of the Jewish people, but those nations who are friendly to the Jews will still exist during the time of the Moshiach as before. Obviously they will accord great honor and respect to God's true, chosen nation. And, like the Jewish nation, their primary occupation will be to understand and become closer to God.

> "They will bring all your brethren from all the nations as an offering to God — with horses and with chariots and with covered wagons and with mules — with joyous dances to My holy mountain, Jerusalem," says God, "just as the children of Israel bring the offering in a pure vessel to the House of God."
>
> (*Yeshayah* 66:20)

> In those days it will happen that ten men of each of the languages of the nations will take hold. They will take hold of the corner of the garment of a Jewish man, saying, "Let us go with you, for we have heard that God is with you."
>
> (*Zechariah* 8:23)

DANIEL: But if the gentiles really believe in God and the Torah, why wouldn't they convert to Judaism?

RABBI COHEN: Because they won't be permitted to convert. In this world, any person who decides to forsake his entire life to become a Jew is allowed to convert. There is no question that becoming a Jew involves at least some degree of difficulty and sacrifice. But once the Moshiach arrives and the world is shown the truth, converts will no longer be accepted out of concern that they are converting for less than altruistic reasons.

There is even a precedent for this idea. During the time of King David, converts were not accepted because they might have joined the Jewish people only because they feared the military might of the kingdom. The same was true during King Shlomo's time, when converts were not accepted out of concern that they were attracted to Israel's might and wealth.[19]

> Our Rabbis have taught: We will not accept converts in the days of the Moshiach. Similarly, they did not accept converts during the time of [King] David or during the time of [King] Shlomo.
>
> (*Yevamos* 24b)

We've pretty much answered your question about the nature of the world during the time of the Moshiach, but there are two additional points I want you to keep in mind. First, although we've mostly discussed the twelfth principle of the Rambam until now, don't forget the ninth. Neither the Moshiach nor anyone else will ever change the Torah in any way. All the mitzvos will still apply during the time of the Moshiach.[20]

> And the ninth principle, the "cancellation." Meaning, that the Torah of Moshe will never be canceled, and there will never come another Torah from God beside it. It will never be added to or subtracted from, neither from the Written Law nor the Oral Law, as it says, "Neither add to it nor subtract from it" (*Devarim* 13:1).
>
> (Rambam, *Peirush HaMishnayos, Sanhedrin, Chelek*)

The second point I want you to keep in mind is that although we've managed to piece together a basic, viable description of the era of the Moshiach, the true reality will certainly defy our imagination. Rav Sa'adyah Gaon proves this with the following idea.

God told Avraham that his descendants would be forced into slavery for a period of four hundred years. He then consoled Avraham with the knowledge that when the Jewish people would finally be redeemed God would give them great wealth and judge the enslaving nation. The redemption from Egypt vastly exceeded God's promise. The nation witnessed such wonders as the ten plagues and the splitting of the sea. Regarding the final redemption, the prophets said that the Jewish nation will receive vast wealth, honor, and many other blessings. And just as God exceeded our expectations of the Exodus, God will exceed our expectations of the final redemption.

> When we were [slaves] in Egypt, [God] only promised us two things [related to the forthcoming redemption], that He would judge our oppressors and that He would give us great wealth. This is the meaning of "But also the nation that they will serve I shall judge, and afterward they will leave with great wealth" (*Bereishis* 15:14). Nevertheless, we witnessed what [God] did for us — the splitting of the sea, the manna, the quail, our standing before Har Sinai, the stopping of the sun [in the heavens] (see *Ta'anis* 20a), and similar events. Certainly since God promised us great and expansive good, wealth, grandeur, splendor, and honor many times greater than the humiliation and oppression that we suffered...God will do to us manifold times greater than what we were promised, an amount that cannot easily be counted and totaled.
>
> (Rav Sa'adyah Gaon, *Emunos V'Deos* 8:1)

DANIEL: Okay, so we said that during the time of the Moshiach the entire creation will revert to the perfect state that would have existed had Adam not transgressed. The laws of nature will remain unchanged, but at the same time the world will undergo tremendous change. Everyone will believe in God and accept the Torah as God's true teaching. The evil inclination will be defeated, and the world will finally achieve peace.

Next we said that people will focus mostly on understanding and becoming close to God, including the gentiles. Also, the Torah and mitzvos will not change during the time of the Moshiach. Finally, we mentioned that the wondrous nature of the world at that time will exceed our hopes and expectations.

RABBI COHEN: Excellent. You're becoming quite an expert on the Moshiach.

DANIEL: Maybe. But there are still a few loose ends. I know — it will have to wait for next week.

Week 7

In which Daniel learns of Armageddon and Eliyahu HaNavi

RABBI COHEN: You said you still have a few questions left. Ask away.

DANIEL: All right. What exactly is the War of Gog U'Magog? Lately I've heard the term mentioned often, but I'm not sure I understand the idea.

RABBI COHEN: It's hard to be very specific about the War of Gog U'Magog because there are so many opinions and ideas involved. Let's talk about what we do understand, though. We know from the words of the prophets that at the time of the redemption a gentile nation will rise against the Land of Israel in an attempt to destroy it. The ensuing war is known as the War of Gog U'Magog, Gog referring to the gentile king and Magog referring to the nation he rules. There are many prophecies concerning the events of the war, including chapters 38 and 39 of *Yechezkel*, 12 and 13 of *Zechariah*, 30 in *Yirmeyah*, and 11 and 12 in *Daniel*. However, there is one underlying theme in the words of the Sages about the war. The trouble and grief of the War of Gog U'Magog will surpass all the troubles we have witnessed in the past.[21]

> "Do not remember the former things or consider the things of old" (*Yeshayah* 43:18). "Do not remember the former things" —

this refers to subjugation by the nations. "Or consider the things of old" — this refers to the Exodus from Egypt. "Behold, I will do a new thing; now it shall spring forth" (*Yeshayah* 43:19). Rav Yosef learned: This refers to the War of Gog U'Magog. To what is this comparable? To a person walking along the way who encountered a wolf and was saved. From then on, he would tell the story of the wolf. Then he encountered a lion and was saved. Thereafter he would tell of the lion. Then he encountered a snake and was saved. He forgot the first two stories and thereafter would tell about the snake. The same is true with Israel. Later troubles make them forget earlier ones.

(*Berachos* 13a)

DANIEL: You said the gentile nation is called Magog. I'll admit that geography's not my strong point, but as far as I know there aren't any kingdoms in today's world that go by that name. So where is it?

RABBI COHEN: When the prophets spoke of Magog, there was in fact a people by that name. However, we no longer know which modern nation descends from Magog. Its true identity will remain unknown until we witness the fulfillment of those prophecies.

The name Gog and the name Magog will already be forgotten in those days to the point where it will be unknown which nation the prophet called Magog and its king, Gog. Only when they come to [conquer] the land and the words of the prophets are fulfilled will we know that this king is the Gog that has been prophesied.

(*Malbim, Yechezkel* 38:17)

DANIEL: How will the war end? I take it the Jewish people will win.

RABBI COHEN: Yes, Gog U'Magog will ultimately be defeated.

What's interesting, though, is the way it will happen. Gog U'Magog will be destroyed in such a miraculous manner that the Jewish nation will not even have to fight the battle.

> I will punish him with pestilence and blood, torrential rain and hailstones; I will rain down fire and sulfur upon him and upon his armies and upon the many nations who are with him.
>
> (*Yechezkel* 38:22)

> They will no longer require weapons, for God fights for them.
>
> (*Malbim, Yechezkel* 39:9)

> In the verses in *Yechezkel*, no mention is made that Moshiach the king and Yisrael will fight with weapons. Rather, God will kill them using "pestilence and blood, torrential rain and hailstones, fire and sulfur."
>
> (*Iggros Moshe, Ohr HaChaim* 4:81)

By the way, it's interesting to note that the final, decisive battle in the War of Gog U'Magog will take place on a mountain called Mount Meggido, or, in Hebrew, Har Meggido. Ever heard the term before?

DANIEL: Hmmm...it sounds familiar. Har Meggido...Har Meggido sounds like...Armageddon?

RABBI COHEN: Right. The place of the apocalyptic ending of Gog U'Magog has become synonymous, in the English language, with any great, destructive battle or event. Another example of God preparing the world for the events of the time of the Moshiach? You never know.

DANIEL: Yeah, that is cool. But there's still something I don't understand. What is the whole war about anyway? I mean, why would God allow another nation to attack Israel at the peak of the redemption?

RABBI COHEN: You've picked up on the salient point — that God will cause the war to occur in the midst of the redemption process, so you already have half of the answer. First, let's recall something we mentioned last week. We said that during the time of the Moshiach, not only will the Jewish people believe in God, but even the whole world will believe. When the Moshiach arrives, it's easy to understand why the Jewish people will laud him as the true redeemer. After all, we've been awaiting him for thousands of years. The gentiles, on the other hand, will be skeptical at best. It will take an event of apocalyptic proportions — excuse the term — to thoroughly convince them of God's existence and the truth that the Jewish people are His chosen nation. That event is the War of Gog U'Magog.

> Behold, a day is coming for God, when your spoils will be divided in your midst. I will gather all the nations to Jerusalem for war.... On that day God will be One and His Name One.
>
> *(Zechariah* 14:1–9)

> Therefore prophesy, son of man, and say to Gog: Thus said the Lord Hashem Elokim, "Surely on that day, when My people, Israel, dwells securely, you will know. When you come from your place in the farthest parts of the north, you and many peoples with you, all of them riding horses, a great horde, a vast army, and you advance against My people, Israel, like a cloud covering the earth. It will be at the end of days that I will bring you upon My land, in order that the nations may know Me, when I become sanctified through you before their eyes, Gog."
>
> *(Yechezkel* 38:14–16)

> Because of the wonders that I do to you [Gog], everyone will recognize My divinity.
>
> *(Malbim,* ad. loc.)

DANIEL: I've also heard that Eliyahu HaNavi is supposed to come sometime before the War of Gog U'Magog. Where does he fit in?

RABBI COHEN: You are correct that Eliyahu HaNavi will come to the Jewish people before the war. According to the overwhelming majority of opinions, he will come some time before the arrival of the Moshiach.[22]

> Behold, I will send you Eliyahu HaNavi before the coming of the great and awesome day of God. And he will turn back [to God] the hearts of fathers with the sons and the hearts of sons with their fathers....
>
> (*Malachi* 3:23)

> There is an opinion of the Sages that states that Eliyahu will come before the arrival of Moshiach the king.
>
> (Rambam, *Hilchos Melachim* 12:2)

DANIEL: What is Eliyahu supposed to do?

RABBI COHEN: There are many reasons Eliyahu is needed. First, he will urge the Jewish nation to repent. We have already discussed the vital connection between repentance and the redemption, so this is no small matter. But the Sages go a step further and explain that the Jewish nation will repent only when Eliyahu arrives.

> Rabbi Yehudah says: If the people of Israel do not repent, they will not be redeemed. And they will repent only amid pain, wandering, and lack of sustenance. They will not repent until Eliyahu arrives, as it says, "Behold, I will send you Eliyahu HaNavi" (*Malachi* 3:23–24), which is followed by "And he will turn back [to God] the hearts of fathers with the sons."
>
> (*Yalkut Shimoni, Malachi* 595)

"And he will turn back [to God] the hearts of fathers" — to the

Holy One, blessed is He. "With the sons" — by means of their sons. He will say to their sons in a loving and persuasive manner, "Go and tell your fathers to take hold of the ways of God."

(Rashi, Malachi 3:23–24)

He will urge the fathers and the sons together to return completely to God.

(Radak, Malachi 3:23–24)

Second, Eliyahu will begin the process of bringing peace to the world.

The Sages, however, say: [Eliyahu is coming] neither to distance [those families known to be invalid yet were accepted by force] nor to accept [those families known to be kosher yet were rejected by force]. Rather [the purpose of his coming] is to make peace in the world....

(Mishnah, Eduyos 8:7)

Also, Eliyahu will clarify halachic uncertainties.

Until Eliyahu arrives and teaches if it is permitted or prohibited.

(Rashi, Bechoros 24a,
s.v. "ad yavo v'yoreh tzeddek lachem")

Finally, we've mentioned that the Moshiach will rule the Jewish nation as a king. In order to be crowned as a Jewish king, a person must first be anointed by a prophet. Eliyahu HaNavi is the prophet who will anoint the Moshiach as king.

On the day that Eliyahu anoints the Moshiach by the commandment of God, he will be called [by the title] "Moshiach."

(Ramban, Sefer HaVikuach 24)

DANIEL: There's still something missing, though. You've explained why we need Eliyahu, but you haven't explained why we need

Eliyahu. Why was Eliyahu chosen from among all the other prophets to come to the Jewish people during the time of the redemption? Why is Eliyahu the one who will answer our halachic questions and help the Jewish nation repent?

> As they were walking and conversing, behold, a chariot of fire and horses of fire [appeared] and separated the two of them, and Eliyahu ascended to Heaven in a whirlwind. Elisha was watching and shouting, "Father! Father! Israel's chariot and horsemen!" And then he saw [Eliyahu] no more. He took hold of his garments and ripped them into two pieces.
>
> (*Melachim* II 2:11)

RABBI COHEN: The prophets tell us that on the day Eliyahu left this world a fiery chariot plucked him from earth and carried him up to the heavens. The Sages explain that Eliyahu did not actually die, but entered Heaven from a living state. In fact, the Sages list nine people who entered Heaven without dying first. Yet Eliyahu is unique in that he does not remain solely in the spiritual realm, but continues to frequent the physical world as well.

DANIEL: Hold on a second. Heaven is a spiritual place, right? So how can a physical body enter the spiritual world? And how can he travel back and forth?

RABBI COHEN: His body underwent a process of refinement as he ascended. In essence, he became quasi-spiritual. Eliyahu is spiritual enough that he can traverse the spiritual realm, yet corporeal enough that he can manifest himself on the earth. The Gemara and Midrash are full of accounts of Eliyahu appearing to the righteous of each generation, offering wisdom and advice as necessary.

If you ever try your hand at Jewish outreach, you'll learn one important fact: In order to bring Jews closer to the Torah and God, it is vital to understand where they are coming from; you need to understand their mentality. Only someone who has experienced the myriad changes in the world over the centuries is capable of bringing the Jewish people closer to God. If God were to resurrect a different prophet, despite his greatness, he could not be the person best equipped for outreach.

DANIEL: I assume it wasn't a coincidence that Eliyahu was available.

RABBI COHEN: Without question. Obviously God prepared such a person expressly for the task of outreach at the time of redemption. The idea is also true of halachic questions. A person can decide matters of halachah only if they understand their generation and its needs. Again, Eliyahu is uniquely positioned for this task.

> At first glance, it is possible to ask...why will Eliyahu resolve difficulties and questions? Moshe Rabbeinu, *alav hashalom*, who gave us the Torah and mitzvos, will rise [during the resurrection]. Why won't he resolve all the difficulties we have with the holy Torah?... Chazal, who lived after the generation of Beis Shammai and Beis Hillel, saw that the world needs to operate through *chesed*. Therefore, they decided that the halachah always follows Beis Hillel's leniencies. Now, who is capable of discerning the attribute through which the world needs to function so that the halachah can be decided accordingly? Only someone who is alive and exists in this world knows which attribute the world requires. Someone who is not alive, however, has no idea which attribute the world requires. Eliyahu, who is alive and exists in this world and has never tasted death, will resolve all the difficulties and questions, for he knows the attribute through which the world needs to function.
>
> (*Kedushas HaLevi, Likutim*, vol. 1, p. 316)

DANIEL: Will he appear only to righteous people, though? Uh...I'm not exactly sure I fall into that category.

RABBI COHEN: Don't worry. When the redemption arrives, God will cause Eliyahu's physical body to "thicken" somewhat, so he will be visible to everyone. After all, outreach is foremost for those distant from God.

> Eliyahu HaNavi will reveal all matters that were hidden in this world. When the other prophets, judges, and wise men, who lived in previous generations — even the patriarchs, the tribes, and all those who lived from the time of Moshe Rabbeinu until the resurrection — come back to life, they will not know what happened in this world after their deaths. They were in the upper and lower Garden of Eden, separated from the concerns of this physical world. But Eliyahu, who lived from the time of Moshe Rabbeinu until the time of Yehoram, knew everything that occurred during his lifetime. Also, after he departed [this world] with body and soul, his body became as purified, if not greater, than one of the celestial bodies. God prepared him to be available in Israel's time of need, so that He could save them through him and in his merit....
>
> Eliyahu, z"l, however, was sustained by God in a pure body and a delicate soul, and [He] chose him from among all the other prophets because He recognized in him a certain readiness for these [levels of] understanding.... He knows all of the lofty matters that occur in the spiritual world because of his refined soul, and he knows everything that occurs in this world because of his pure body. For even though he is delicate and pure, he retains a small amount — in quantity and quality — of physicality, which is undetectable in [physical] circumstances and movements....
>
> Even though he lives in the way we described, at the time

of the resurrection he will experience a pseudo-resurrection. His body will thicken somewhat and become more physical, making him visible to all of the redeemed and resurrected people and enabling him to dwell permanently among them and act as they do....

Even Moshe Rabbeinu, through whom the Torah was given, will not be able to clarify the uncertainties of the Torah, even though they are clear to him. This is so because when God brings him back to life, he will speak as if from the heavens, since his soul was separated from his body. But the verse says, "It [the Torah] is not in the heavens" (*Devarim* 30:12)....

(*Beis Elokim, Sha'ar HaYesodos* 60)

DANIEL: All right, next question. The ten tribes — they're coming back, right?

RABBI COHEN: Sort of.

DANIEL: Sort of?

RABBI COHEN: Let's start from the beginning. We know that the ten tribes — every tribe with the exception of Yehudah and Binyamin — were exiled by Shalmaneser, the king of Assyria, during the time of the first Beis HaMikdash.

In the ninth year of [the reign of] Hoshea, the king of Assyria captured Samaria and exiled Israel to Assyria. He settled them in Halah, in Habor, by the Gozan River, and in the cities of Media.

(*Melachim* II 17:6)

The Mishnah records a disagreement between Rabbi Akiva and Rabbi Eliezer about the future of the ten tribes. Rabbi Eliezer stated that they will return to the Jewish people during the time of the redemption. Rabbi Akiva, however, was of the opinion that the tribes that went into exile will never return.

> The ten tribes are not destined to return [from exile], as it says, "And He cast them to another land, as today" (*Devarim* 29:27) — just as the day goes, never to return, so they went, never to return. These are the words of Rabbi Akiva. Rabbi Eliezer says: "As today" — just as the day darkens and then becomes light, so too the ten tribes, for whom it is dark, will also have light one day.
>
> (*Sanhedrin* 110b)

DANIEL: But how can that be? You've told me that one of the primary tasks of the Moshiach will be to gather the exiles from every corner of the earth. According to Rabbi Akiva, the Moshiach will redeem twelve tribes — except for ten. That's like saying, "A car, except for its engine, chassis, and wheels." There isn't enough left to call it a car.

RABBI COHEN: That's a good question. You must keep in mind, though, that the Moshiach will only redeem the Jewish people from the exile. According to Rabbi Akiva, the Jews who were exiled by the king of Assyria have been gone for so long that they have assimilated into the gentile nations. I'm not referring to Jews who no longer keep the Torah, but to Jews who have intermarried for so many generations that their descendants are no longer halachically Jewish. They cannot be redeemed because they are gentiles.

DANIEL: If it's a simple argument between Rabbi Akiva and Rabbi Eliezer, why did you answer, "Sort of," when I asked you if the ten tribes will return?

RABBI COHEN: Because despite the basic argument, there are two important facts they both agree on. First, both agree that only the majority of the ten tribes were exiled in the first place. Try to imagine the exile and you'll understand. A portion of the Jews would have escaped the armies of Shalmaneser. Another group might have been visiting the lands of Yehudah and Binyamin. Others might have been outside Eretz Yisrael temporarily. So there is no question that the Jewish nation has always contained twelve tribes, though nowadays we don't really know who belongs to which tribe.

> Nevertheless, the opinion of Rabbi Akiva, as is true, is that despite the fact that most of the [ten] tribes were exiled and taken by the king of Assyria to Halah, Habor, the Gozan River, and the cities of Media, not every single person was taken. For in the conquering of a nation, it is impossible that many did not escape, flee, and leave in every direction. The Sages already mentioned that during their exile many people from the [ten] tribes went with Chizkiyahu and settled in the cities of Yehudah. Referring to this, Yeshayahu said, "What will the messengers of the nations say? That God has established Zion, and in it the poor of His people take shelter" (*Yeshayah* 14:32).
>
> (Abarbanel, *Yeshuos Meshicho* 1:4)

The second point that both Rabbi Akiva and Rabbi Eliezer agree on is that a portion of the ten tribes that were exiled already returned to the Jewish people during the time of Yirmeyahu the prophet.

> Rabbi Yochanan said: Yirmeyah was not there, for he had gone to retrieve the ten tribes. And how do we know that they returned? Because it says [referring to *yovel*], "For the seller shall not return to the sale" (*Yechezkel* 7:13). Is it possible that [after the observance of] *yovel* was suspended, the prophet would

prophesy that it would be suspended [in the future]? Rather, this teaches that Yirmeyahu retrieved [the ten tribes, and the observance of *yovel*, which can be kept only when all twelve tribes are living in Eretz Yisrael, in fact resumed. Yechezkel's prophecy referred to the distant future when the observance of *yovel* would again be suspended].

(*Megillah* 14b)

When the Gemara says that Yirmeyah returned [the ten tribes to Eretz Yisrael], it does not mean that he returned them all. Rather, he returned a portion.

(*Rashi, Sanhedrin* 110b, s.v. *"ein asidin lachzor"*)

Therefore, both Rabbi Akiva and Rabbi Eliezer agree that during the time of the Moshiach there will be twelve tribes. The argument between them is only regarding whether those who were exiled were lost among the gentiles.

There is no argument regarding whether the ten tribes will exist in the future, or only Yehudah and Binyamin, for it is impossible that one tribe will be missing from Israel, God forbid.

(Maharal, *Netzach Yisrael* 34)

DANIEL: So according to both opinions the Jewish nation will have twelve tribes. That sure changes the simple meaning of the text.

RABBI COHEN: Which is exactly one of the points I made when we first talked about the Moshiach. On the surface, it seems like there are no clear-cut answers to many of our questions about the Moshiach; everything seems to be a disagreement. Yet if we scratch the surface, we find a wealth of knowledge and clarity. Of course, there is still much that remains unclear. What is amazing, though, is the amount of light the Sages did shed on the subject.

DANIEL: One final question. I don't know what this means, but I've heard that there are really two Moshiachs. Is that true?

RABBI COHEN: Absolutely. There is an accepted tradition discussed by the Sages and the *Rishonim* that there will be not one but two Moshiachs. The Moshiach we've been discussing, the one referred to in most places, is Moshiach ben David, a descendant of King David, as we explained. There will also be a Moshiach ben Yosef, a descendant of Yosef, who will precede Moshiach ben David. Occasionally the Sages also refer to him as Moshiach ben Efraim.

> "God showed me four craftsmen" (*Zechariah* 2:3). Who are these "four craftsmen"? Rav Channa bar Bizna said in the name of Rabbi Shimon Chasidah: [They are] Moshiach ben David, Moshiach ben Yosef, Eliyahu, and "the priest of righteousness" [referring to Shem, son of Noach].
>
> (*Sukkah* 52b)

> Because of Yehoshua your servant, head of the *Sanhedrin*. In the future, Eretz Yisrael will be apportioned through him, Moshiach ben Efraim will descend from him, and the House of Israel will achieve victory through him over Gog and his host at the end of days.
>
> (*Targum Yonasan, Shemos* 40:11)

Everything we've discussed until this point, such as the ingathering of the exiles and the rebuilding of the Beis HaMikdash, are all tasks associated with Moshiach ben David. Moshiach ben Yosef, who will arrive first, has one primary task to perform: he will lead the Jewish nation in the wars that accompany the birth pangs of the Moshiach, including the War of Gog U'Magog. According to the Abarbanel, the reason Rabbi Akiva believed Bar Kochva was the Moshiach was only because he thought he was Moshiach ben Yosef.

Because it was an accepted tradition among the [Jewish] nation that Moshiach ben Yosef will precede Moshiach ben David. He will not come to perform justice and charity, but solely to fight the wars of God and to take vengeance on their oppressors.

(Abarbanel, *Yeshuos Meshicho* 1:4)

DANIEL: I'm still missing something, though. Why do we need a second Moshiach at all? We've discussed why the Moshiach must come from King David — God promised that his descendants would rule forever and thus the Moshiach will rule as a king. But why do we need a second — or, rather, first — Moshiach who descends from Yosef? Couldn't Moshiach ben David fight the wars himself?

RABBI COHEN: The Sages explain that the descendants of Esav, meaning Rome and its cultural descendants, in whose exile we now live, will be defeated only by a descendant of Yosef. This complements the idea we just mentioned, that the primary task of Moshiach ben Yosef is to fight the wars. Once Esav is defeated, Moshiach ben David will assume the task of our spiritual redemption, as we explained in the very first week. I don't mean that Moshiach ben Yosef will purposely instigate a war. But he will defend the Jewish people from any hostile nation.

Yaakov saw that Esav's descendants could be defeated only by Yosef's descendants.

(*Bava Basra* 123b)

In whose hands shall Edom fall? Those of the "Moshiach of war," who descends from Yosef.

(*Bereishis Rabbah* 99:2)

DANIEL: But why will Esav fall only to the descendants of Yosef?

RABBI COHEN: We know that Yaakov purchased the firstborn

blessings from Esav and ultimately received them from Yitzchak. As part of the blessings, Yaakov was given the right to rule over his sibling. The Maharsha explains that when Yaakov in turn blessed his own children, he passed on this right to Yosef alone. Therefore only the children of Yosef will be able to defeat Edom, the descendants of Esav.

> This means that with the purchase of the birthright and the taking of the blessings by Yaakov from Esav, he earned dominion over Esav his elder. Yaakov passed all of this to Yosef, as it says in the [Gemara's] discussion, "And I have given you Shechem — one portion more than your brothers — which I took from the hand of the Emori with my sword and with my bow" (*Bereishis* 48:22). Thus the descendants of Esav will be defeated only by [the descendants of] Yosef and not the rest of the brothers.
>
> (*Maharsha, Bava Basra* 123b)

DANIEL: Do we know anything specific about the life of Moshiach ben Yosef?

RABBI COHEN: The Sages tell us that the era of Moshiach ben Yosef will be a time of great peril and persecution for the Jewish nation, culminating in the death of Moshiach ben Yosef during the battle against Gog U'Magog.

> "They will look toward Me because of those whom they have stabbed; they will mourn him as one mourns an only child" (*Zechariah* 12:10). Why is there a eulogy? There was a disagreement between Rabbi Dosa and the Rabbis. One said [the prophecy refers to the eulogy that will take place] upon Moshiach ben Yosef's death.
>
> (*Sukkah* 52a)

They also said that the catalyst for this will be the rise of a man who is a descendant of Yosef in Har HaGalil. He will gather the remnants of the [Jewish] nation and turn [his attention] to the Holy Temple, since Edom has taken hold of it. He will live there for a while, and afterward a man named Armelius will fight them and conquer the city, kill and take captives, and the man from Yosef will be slain. The nation will be beset by great troubles at that time, the harshest of which will be the breakdown of relations between the Jewish people and all the nations [to the point that the nations] will banish them to the desert....

(Rav Sa'adyah Gaon, *Emunos V'Deos* 8:5)

DANIEL: So he's going to die?

RABBI COHEN: Possibly. This is yet another example of the principle that events during the era of the Moshiach depend on the manner in which the redemption arrives. If the redemption occurs because the Jewish nation repents of their own accord, it is possible that the time of troubles will be avoided entirely. Otherwise, Moshiach ben Yosef will die during the war. Then Moshiach ben David will finally arrive. He will rescue the Jewish people and defeat the forces of Gog U'Magog. The redemption will then proceed as we discussed.

I will explain the two situations together. Meaning, if we do not return [to God in repentance], the events of Moshiach ben Yosef [and the era preceding his arrival] will occur. And if we return [to God] and exempt ourselves from those events, Moshiach ben David will immediately be revealed. If Moshiach ben Yosef has already preceded him, he will act as Moshiach ben David's messenger and a guide to the nation to clear the way for his arrival. And if Moshiach ben Yosef has not arrived, Moshiach ben David will still be revealed immediately [meaning, there will be no need for Moshiach ben Yosef], as it says,

117

"Suddenly, the master whom you seek will come to His Sanctuary."

(Rav Sa'adyah Gaon, *Emunos V'Deos* 8:6)

DANIEL: Wow! We've covered a lot of ground. Let me try to sum up what we've learned. At the time of the redemption, a gentile king known as Gog will attempt to conquer the Land of Israel. That war will be known as the War of Gog U'Magog. Ultimately Gog and his nation will be defeated in a miraculous way, and those very miracles will finally prove God's existence to the world.

We know that Eliyahu HaNavi will arrive sometime before the War of Gog U'Magog. Like the Moshiach, Eliyahu has specific tasks to perform, including helping the Jewish nation to repent, clarifying our halachic questions, and anointing the Moshiach as king. We explained why Eliyahu is uniquely suited for the job, and the basic idea is this: since he never died, he understands the needs of our modern world.

We also talked about the ten tribes. Rabbi Akiva and Rabbi Eliezer argued about whether their descendants will ultimately return, but they agreed on two things. First, they agreed that only the majority of the ten tribes were exiled; a certain percentage escaped that fate and remained with the Jewish people. Second, they agree that a portion of the ten tribes already returned to the Jewish nation. So, no matter what, there will definitely be twelve tribes in the future.

Finally, we said that there are really two Moshiachs, Moshiach ben David and Moshiach ben Yosef. Moshiach ben Yosef, who will arrive first, will begin the process of redemption by fighting the wars that take place during the redemption. Afterward, Moshiach ben David will arrive to complete the redemption.

RABBI COHEN: Excellent! Just keep in mind that the Moshiach we referred to in the preceding weeks is Moshiach ben David. Although Moshiach ben Yosef will fight against hostile nations, their ultimate defeat will come only at the hands of Moshiach ben David (week 1). And we mentioned that if a person dies before accomplishing the designated tasks, we know that he was not the Moshiach (week 2). Again, that was referring to Moshiach ben David. Moshiach ben Yosef, as we said, may be killed.

Surely you must be running low on questions, my friend.

DANIEL: I hate to admit it, but yeah, you've pretty much answered all of my questions about the Moshiach.

RABBI COHEN: Hate to admit it? Wasn't that the point?

DANIEL: Sure. These sessions have kind of grown on me, though. I do still have some questions about the distant future — the resurrection of the dead and the World to Come, but I suppose they're not directly related to the Moshiach. I don't suppose...

RABBI COHEN: That I'd have time to discuss them? Of course. You might be surprised how related the ideas are. Next week?

DANIEL: Great. I'll see you then.

Week 8

In which Daniel learns of futures near and far

RABBI COHEN: So you wanted to ask about the resurrection.

DANIEL: Right. The resurrection of the dead. What's it all about?

RABBI COHEN: Let's start with the basics. We know that sometime in the future a momentous event known as the resurrection of the dead will occur. While a person is alive, he exists as a composite of two opposite elements, a body and soul. When he dies, the body decomposes, but his soul lives on in the spiritual realm. During the resurrection of the dead, his body will be reunited with its soul, and the person will live again.

> The resurrection of the dead means the return of the soul to the body after [their separation at] death.
>
> (Rambam, *Iggeres Techiyas HaMeisim* 2)

The Sages quote many verses that explicitly mention, or allude to, the event. And for those who have difficulty with the basic concept of the dead rising, the Sages mention an additional proof: the prophets Eliyahu, Elisha, and Yechezkel have already performed acts of resurrection. According to the Rambam, belief in the resurrection of the dead is one of the thirteen fundamental tenets of Judaism.

See now that I, I am He, and no god is with Me. I will put to death, and I will bring to life.

(*Devarim* 32:39)

May Your dead come to life; may my corpses arise. Awake and sing joyously, you who rest in the dirt!

(*Yeshayah* 26:19)

If a person asks you, "Is it really possible that the Holy One, blessed is He, will resurrect the dead in the future?" reply to him that it has already occurred. The dead were already resurrected by Eliyahu, Elisha, and Yechezkel.

(*Midrash Rabbah, Koheles* 3:15)

Furthermore, I will say that God is aware of the thoughts that will enter our hearts concerning the improbability of resurrecting the dead. Therefore, God preempted this and told his prophet Yechezkel, "Son of man, these bones — they are the whole House of Israel. Behold, they are saying, 'Our bones are dried out, and our hope is lost; we are doomed' " (*Yechezkel* 37:11).

(Rav Sa'adyah Gaon, *Emunos V'Deos* 7:2)

The resurrection of the dead is one of the basic tenets of the Torah of Moshe Rabbeinu.

(Rambam, *Peirush HaMishnayos, Sanhedrin, Chelek*)

DANIEL: When is the resurrection going to happen?

RABBI COHEN: Obviously I have no exact dates for you, so we'll have to stick to the general principles. The first point you have to know is that according to many opinions there are actually going to be two resurrections of the dead.

DANIEL: Two?

RABBI COHEN: That's right. The first will occur relatively soon after the arrival of the Moshiach. Only people who were completely righteous during their lifetime, such as the forefathers and Moshe Rabbeinu, will rise. A second, general resurrection will take place at the end of the era of the Moshiach. Everyone who ever lived, whether righteous or evil, will rise at that time to be judged by God. Those deemed worthy will pass to the final state of the world, which we'll discuss in a moment, while those judged evil will receive appropriate punishment.

> Many of those who sleep in the dusty earth will awaken: these for everlasting life and those for shame, for everlasting abhorrence.
>
> (*Daniel* 12:2)

> The resurrection of the dead...in this world [by Eliyahu, Elisha, and Yechezkel] occurred in order to sanctify His great Name. There will also be a resurrection of the dead during the days of the son of David in order to reward those who love and fear Him. There will also be a resurrection of the dead in the World to Come, in order to give judgment and reckoning, as it says, "May Your dead come to life; may my corpses arise. Awake and sing joyously, you who rest in the dirt! For your dew is like the dew that [revives] vegetation; may you topple the lifeless [wicked] to the ground" (*Yeshayah* 26:19).
>
> (*Tanna D'Bei Eliyahu* 5:5)

I saw the words of the Ritva, z"l, in the name of his masters, may their souls rest, that there are two resurrections. One is a specific resurrection for the righteous who died in the exile, which will occur immediately after the arrival of the Moshiach. They will merit [life during] the entire era of the Moshiach with body and soul, and they will experience the goodness of Israel and the rebuilding of the Beis HaMikdash, and they will rejoice over the rewards of their service [to God].... And one is a general resurrection, which is close to the "onset of Shabbos," according to the tradition I received. That period of time is called "the world of the resurrection," about which it is said, "Many of those who sleep in the dusty earth will awaken" (*Daniel* 12:2).

(Radbaz, Responsa 3:1069)

Therefore, they said that there are two resurrections, a specific one for those righteous people who died in the exile...and a general one at the end of the sixth millennium. The scholars of Kabbalah also agreed and the Ramban, the Rashba, and the Ritva....

(Radbaz, *Migdal David*, p. 83a)

DANIEL: I'm missing something, though. You've told me what the resurrection is and when it's going to happen. But why do we need it? How does the resurrection fit into the bigger picture?

RABBI COHEN: Listen carefully, because you'll get confused if you're not paying attention. To understand the underlying idea of the resurrection, you need to view it within the context of a second concept. There is a fundamental argument between the Rambam and a group of *Rishonim* and *Geonim* — Rav Sa'adyah Gaon, the Ramban, and at least five others — concerning the final state of mankind's existence. The Rambam was of the opinion that the ultimate state of being, what most people think of as "Heaven" or "*Olam HaBa*," is purely spiritual. Meaning, we will exist as incorporeal souls, without a body of any kind.

In the World to Come, there are no [physical] bodies or substance, but rather the righteous alone without bodies, like the ministering angels. Since there will be no bodies, there will be no eating, drinking, or any other requirement of the body in this world.

(Rambam, *Hilchos Teshuvah* 8:2)

DANIEL: One second. Didn't we just say that during the resurrection of the dead each soul will be rejoined with its body?

RABBI COHEN: Absolutely. But according to the Rambam, the period of the resurrection is temporary. Eventually everyone will die once again and pass on to the final state, *Olam HaBa* — a state of soul alone.[23]

The vast majority disagreed with the Rambam. They argued that our final state of being is a union of a physical body and spiritual soul, similar to our existence today.

DANIEL: You know, I never even knew there was an argument about this. Who would have thought the Rambam is the minority opinion?

RABBI COHEN: You're certainly not alone, and it's not too difficult to imagine why most people think as you did. Obviously it is not for us to *pasken* — to decide in favor of one of the two opinions — but since Rav Sa'adyah Gaon and the Ramban represent the vast majority, we'll limit our discussion to their opinions.[24]

DANIEL: Sounds good.

RABBI COHEN: Now if we apply what we just learned to your question, we can understand the significance of the resurrection of the dead. Since the final state of existence is body and soul joined together, the resurrection is necessary to rejoin our two components so we can pass on to the final state of the world.

The reward for souls and their existence in the World of Souls is called "Gan Eden" by our Masters, and sometimes "*aliyah*" or "*yeshivah shel malah.*" Afterward comes the era of the Moshiach, which is still considered part of this world. At the end [of the era of the Moshiach] will be the Day of Judgment and the resurrection of the dead, which [will lead to the ultimate] reward for the body and soul. The primary reward [for serving God] and the aspiration of all those who hope in the Holy One, blessed is He, is the World to Come. There the body will become as purified as the soul, and the soul will attain lofty wisdom.

(Ramban, *Sha'ar HaGemul* 346)

The implication is that it is impossible that we will not have bodies in the World to Come, where the righteous receive their reward and the wicked are repaid [for their transgressions]. This straightforward tradition, known by the entire Jewish nation, has been passed down, individual after individual, as a tradition [transmitted] to Moshe from [the divine revelation at] Sinai. All the *Geonim* wrote similarly in their writings, including Rav Sa'adyah in his *Sefer Emunos*. It is also logical, for just as the attribute of justice dictates that the soul be rewarded for its uprightness and be repaid for its virtue, so too the attribute of justice dictates that the body be rewarded for its uprightness and be repaid for its virtue....

(*Yad Ramah, Sanhedrin* 90a,
s.v. "*v'inyan*")

DANIEL: So the purpose of the resurrection is to reunite our body and soul. But why did God create the world like this? Each person has to live, die, then be resurrected. Why do we have to die? Why didn't God make people live forever?

RABBI COHEN: If you remember, a couple of weeks ago (week 6) we spoke about Adam HaRishon and the creation of the world. In brief, we mentioned that when Adam transgressed and ate from the tree, he caused a destructive change to take place in the world. Let's take a close look at one aspect of that change.

The Sages tell us that man was created for the sole purpose of basking in, and receiving pleasure from, the Presence of God. Since God is purely spiritual, that pleasure is also of a spiritual nature. This presents a difficulty, though. We've explained that the final state of our existence is with both body and soul, as we live today. Yet now we're saying that we were created to receive pleasure from the Presence of God, which is a spiritual pleasure. How does a physical body experience spiritual sensations?

The answer is, in a word, the soul. The soul has many functions, some that we recognize and some that we hardly realize exist. When man was first created, his soul had a special function. It was meant to purify his body to such an extent that even the physical half would experience the pleasure of being close to God. Our description of Eliyahu HaNavi last week (week 7) should give you an idea of the type of perfection we're talking about. He purified himself to such a degree that he was able to enter Heaven alive. The goal is for the body to become so purified that it scarcely resembles the physicality we recognize at all.

If Adam had not transgressed, he would have been able to reach this awesome level of perfection. Adam did transgress, however, and this relationship between the body and soul was lost. In the present, damaged state of the world, the soul can no longer completely purify the body as it was meant to do.

In order for the soul to regain this ability, in order for the true relationship between the body and soul to be reinstated, everything that was corrupted must be destroyed and remade once more. Therefore, man must die and be reborn in a form that is once again capable of attaining this form of perfection.

You must know that we are aware of the soul's effect on the body only because it provides us with life and the ability to think. However, the soul also has another function, to purify man's physical body, gradually elevating it until it, too, can receive pleasure from perfection along with the soul. Had Adam not sinned, this is the level he would have attained. His soul would have gradually purified his body until he reached the level required to partake of the everlasting bliss.

When Adam sinned, things were greatly changed.... Besides this, God decreed that neither man nor the world would be able to attain perfection while still in the corrupted form, meaning the present state, in which the evil has increased. Therefore, man, and everything else that was ruined with him, must pass through a period of destruction, meaning death. The soul cannot purify the body until the body dies and deteriorates and a new structure is composed — one that the soul can enter and purify.

(Ramchal, Derech Hashem I:3:7–8)

DANIEL: But let's say Adam had never sinned in the first place? Are you saying that if he hadn't sinned, he never would have died?

RABBI COHEN: Absolutely. When Adam was originally created, he was meant to live forever. It was the transgression — the damage wrought on his body, soul, and the creation at large — that introduced the need for death in the world.

God commanded the man saying, "You may eat from every tree of the garden. But of the Tree of Knowledge of Good and Evil you may not eat, for on the day you eat of it you will surely die."[25]

(Bereishis 2:16–17)

According to our Masters, if [Adam HaRishon] had not

transgressed, he never would have died, for his lofty soul would have provided eternal life.

(Ramban, ad. loc.; see also Shabbos 55a)

DANIEL: But you still haven't explained why we will need a body. Sure, the soul will purify the body so that it can also experience spiritual pleasure. What's the point, though? Why won't we exist as a soul alone and forget the body?

RABBI COHEN: An excellent question. Since it seems our body is meant only to provide for our physical needs in this world, why do we need it in our final state of existence? Ultimately, our bodies will become so refined that we will no longer eat or drink anyway. So why the need for a body?

There are two answers to your question. First, the Sages explained that just as the soul is rewarded for its actions in this world, so too the body must be rewarded. And since the body and soul were joined while they served God, it is logical that they be reunited to receive their due.

> Antoninus said to Rebbi: "The body and soul are [seemingly] able to excuse themselves from judgment. How? The body claims that the soul sinned 'because from the day it separated from me, I have been lying like a silent rock in the grave.' The soul claims that the body sinned 'because from the day I separated from it, I have been flying in the air like a bird [incapable of transgression].' [Therefore, neither the body nor the soul should be punished.]" Rebbi answered: "I will give you a parable. To what can this be compared? To a human king who owned a beautiful orchard that contained beautiful figs. He stationed two guards [there], one lame and one blind. The lame one said to the blind one, 'Come, mount me [on your shoulders], and we will retrieve [the figs] and eat them.' The lame

one mounted the blind one, and they retrieved and ate them. Later the owner of the orchard arrived. He asked, 'Where are the beautiful figs?' The lame one answered, 'Do I have feet with which to go [and get the figs]?' The blind one answered, 'Do I have eyes with which to see?' What did [the king] do? He placed the lame one on top of the blind one and judged them as one. So, too, God brings the soul and places it in the body and judges them as one...."

(*Sanhedrin* 91a)

You might ask, won't these vessels [limbs and organs] ultimately be useless? They will not be useless, for just as the body and soul were united as they labored to fulfill the mitzvos, so too the body and soul will be rewarded as one. God does not withhold the reward of any creature.

(Rabbeinu Bachyai, *Devarim* 30:15)

Briefly stated, the general idea of the resurrection is simple. The Holy One, blessed is He, created man as body and soul together to perform the holy service by keeping the Torah and the mitzvos He gave them. Therefore, it is fitting that they also receive their eternal reward together. It is inconceivable that the body not benefit from its labor, for the Holy One, blessed is He, does not withhold the reward of any creature.

(Ramchal, *Da'as Tevunos* 68)

The Ramban mentions a second reason for the existence of the body. He answers that the underlying premise of our question was mistaken. We assumed that since the physical structure of the body seems geared toward sustenance, therefore that must be its only function. In fact, every facet of the structure of the body contains deep secrets, many of which are either unknown or beyond our comprehension. The stomach and intestines may appear to function exclusively as digestive organs, but there are other, sublime reasons for their existence. And for those reasons, God desires that we exist with a physical body.

> Furthermore, the [human] form contains many deep secrets, for the creation of this particular form was certainly not without rhyme or reason.
>
> (Ramban, *Sha'ar HaGemul* 336)

DANIEL: What about people who happen to be alive when the second, general resurrection arrives? According to what you've said, a person needs to die in order to be remade. So what happens to people who are alive at the time?

RABBI COHEN: Those who are alive at the time of the general resurrection require the same perfection as everyone else. Therefore, they will also die and be immediately resurrected.

> "I shall put to death and I shall bring to life" (*Devarim* 32:39) — until now death has come from the *Sitra Achara*; from here on, I shall put to death and bring to life. From here [we learn] that at the time [of the resurrection of the dead], all those who have not tasted death will be put to death by God and rise immediately. Why? In order that no trace of the taint [of Adam HaRishon's transgression] remain in the world....
>
> (*Zohar*, vol. 2, p. 108b [Vilna edition])

However, everyone who is alive [at the time of the resurrection of the dead] must die and return to dust for at least a short period before the resurrection. Those who are worthy of being resurrected will then be brought back to life.

> (Ramchal, *Ma'amar HaIkarim*, "BaGeulah";
> see also Radbaz, Responsa 2:839)

DANIEL: There's still one important fact you haven't explained. Our soul goes up to Heaven when we die to await the resurrection. But our body goes six feet under. So how does God recombine our decomposed body and soul? I know that God can do whatever He wants. Do we know anything about the mechanics of the resurrection, though?

RABBI COHEN: The Sages explain that every human skeleton contains a unique bone known as the *luz*. This *luz*, a tiny bone located at the base of the vertebrae, never decomposes. In fact, it cannot be destroyed by any force. So while the majority of the body is absorbed into the earth, God will reconstruct it using the *luz* — not very difficult to imagine in an era when scientists know that a microscopic string of DNA contains the entire blueprint of a human being. As you said, God could perform the resurrection in whatever manner He chooses. It's possible that God chose to use the *luz* as a starting point to make the resurrection easier for us to understand and believe.[26]

> Andrianus, may his bones rot, asked Rabbi Yehoshua ben Chananiah, "From where will the Holy One, blessed is He, cause man to sprout [during the resurrection of the dead] in the World to Come?" He replied, "From the *luz* of the spine." Andrianus asked, "How do you know this?" Rabbi Yehoshua replied, "Bring me [a *luz*], and I will show you." They ground it with a grindstone, but it could not be ground. They burned it with fire, but it was not scorched. They soaked it in water, but it did not dissolve. They placed it on an anvil and began to strike it with a hammer, but the anvil cracked and the hammer split, and the *luz* remained whole.
>
> (*Midrash Rabbah, Bereishis* 28:3)

DANIEL: Okay, so far, so good. Tell me about the people who will be resurrected. Will they be regular human beings, like you and me?

RABBI COHEN: Physiologically they will be normal humans — with one exception. They will eat, drink, marry, and procreate like everyone else. Their single occupation, as for everyone during the era of the Moshiach, will be to learn Torah and serve God. But clearly they will be on a different plane of spirituality than we are. This is because they will no longer possess an evil inclination, as we discussed last week (week 7). But the people who rise during the specific resurrection will also be different from the people who will already be alive during the era of the Moshiach and the resurrection. Since those who rise have already passed through the stage of death and reconstruction, their souls will act to elevate them spiritually in a greater way than the others.

> A person might ask whether or not those who live in this world [during the era of the Moshiach] will eat, drink, and marry. We must know that they will eat and drink and marry like us....
>
> (Rav Sa'adyah Gaon, *Emunos V'Deos* 7:5)

DANIEL: So what's the exception?

RABBI COHEN: If you think about it, you'll realize that you already know the answer.

DANIEL: Oh! Of course! They won't die.

RABBI COHEN: Exactly. As we explained, the need for death was created only because the sin of Adam HaRishon corrupted the relationship between the body and soul. Since the people who rise at the resurrection have already experienced death and reconstruction, there is no need for them to repeat the process.

> It was taught in the academy of Eliyahu: The righteous that the Holy One, blessed is He, will resurrect in the future will not return to dust, as it says, "And it shall come to pass that the

remnant will be in Zion and the leftover will be in Jerusalem. 'Holy' shall be said of him; everyone inscribed for life shall be in Jerusalem" (*Yeshayah* 4:3).

(*Sanhedrin* 92a)

But the tradition has revealed to us that those who are resurrected at the time of the redemption will never die. This is also what our predecessors said: "The righteous that the Holy One, blessed is He, will resurrect in the future will not return to dust...."

(Rav Sa'adyah Gaon, *Emunos V'Deos* 7:5)

It is clear from this, that the righteous whom the Holy One, blessed is He, resurrects in the future will not die at all. Rather, they will live a long life with body and soul, and they will utilize their senses for the service of the Creator. In the seventh millennium their flesh and bodies will be purified as Eliyahu or Chanoch or nearly so....

(Radbaz, Responsa 2:839)

DANIEL: Will the people who are resurrected look like they did during life? If I'm still around, will I recognize my family and friends?

RABBI COHEN: Yes, those who are resurrected will look as they had during life, so you'll be able to recognize your friends and family among them. There is one difference, though — for the better. Immediately after the resurrection, those who were sick will be cured of whatever diseases or ailments they had during life.

Then the sight of the blind will be restored, and the hearing of the deaf will be opened. Then the lame man will skip like a gazelle, and the tongue of the mute will sing joyously.

(*Yeshayah* 35:5–6)

They will rise with their blemishes and then be healed.

(*Sanhedrin* 91b)

A person returns [to this world during the resurrection of the dead] in the same way that he goes [to the Next World]. If he goes blind, he returns blind; deaf, he returns deaf. The Holy One, blessed is He, said, "They shall rise as they went, and afterward I will heal them."

(Bereishis Rabbah 9:5)

A person might ask whether they will recognize their beloved ones and relatives, and whether they will recognize one another. I have investigated and found it to be true, for the leaders [who are resurrected] must certainly be recognizable among the nation.

(Rav Sa'adyah Gaon, *Emunos V'Deos* 7:7)

DANIEL: So let me get this straight. First the Moshiach arrives, then the first resurrection of the dead, followed by the era of the Moshiach, then the second resurrection, and finally the Day of Judgment. *Olam HaBa* is next?

RABBI COHEN: Yes, *Olam HaBa* is the next and final stage of the world. But it will not commence immediately after the Day of Judgment. The Sages explain that following the final resurrection and the Day of Judgment, the world will undergo a cataclysmic change as it metamorphoses into its final state. For a period of one thousand years, the world will return to *"tohu vavohu,"* the same nothingness that existed before God created the world. At the end of that time, the world will be remade into a new form, the permanent state of *Olam HaBa*.[27]

> Rav Katina said: The world will exist for six thousand years [followed by] one thousand [years] of destruction, as it says, "God alone will be exalted on that day" (*Yeshayah* 2:11).
>
> (*Sanhedrin* 97a)

I have already written that this is the opinion of our Masters, z"l, and this is the tradition they had possessed on the matter. "Rav Katina said: The world will exist for six thousand years [followed by] one thousand [years] of destruction"...and we don't find anyone in the Talmud disagreed with him.

(Rashba, Responsa 1:9)

After those who are worthy are prepared for eternal existence, each one on their level, the world will be returned to a state of "*tohu vavohu*" [desolation and emptiness]. Meaning, it will lose its form and will return to a state of "water in water," as it was at the beginning of Creation.... The world will then be renewed in a new form that will be fitting for its eternal state.

(Ramchal, *Ma'amar HaIkarim*, "*BaGeulah*")

DANIEL: But what will happen to everyone in the world during the period of destruction?

RABBI COHEN: Keep in mind that those people will be the righteous ones who survive the Day of Judgment. During the next thousand years, they will rise to increasingly higher levels of spirituality. Mankind has never attained such lofty heights, so we have no real terms to describe them. Suffice it to say that they will continue the purification process we've described and continue to move closer and closer to God. Their physical bodies will be purified to the extent that the destruction of the world will neither harm nor affect them.

If you ask, "During those years that God, blessed is He, is destined to renew His world, as it says, 'God alone will be exalted on that day' (*Yeshayah* 2:11) — what will the righteous be doing?" God, blessed is He, will make them wings like the eagles, and they will glide [unharmed] over the surface of the water, as it says, "Therefore we shall not fear when the earth is transformed and when the mountains collapse in the heart of the seas" (*Tehillim* 46:3). And you might say, "They will suffer pain." [Therefore] the verse says, "Those who hope in God shall have renewed strength; they shall sprout wings like eagles. They shall run and not be weary; they shall walk and not be faint" (*Yeshayah* 40:31).

(Sanhedrin 92b)

"Wings" means that the soul will become angelical [i.e., it will become progressively more spiritual]. The body will also [cling to the soul and become purified through it]. They will not be destroyed like the elements [of the world during the destruction].

(Ramban, Sha'ar HeGemul 332)

Chazal taught us that the world will exist for six thousand years followed by a seventh millennium of destruction, after which God, blessed is He, will renew the world. We also find they said, "What will the righteous be doing? God, blessed is He, will make them wings, and they will glide [unharmed] over the surface of the water...."

From the simple meaning of these words we learn that there are three eras: six thousand years, the seventh millennium, and the renewal of the world. For six thousand years the world will exist as it does today. During the seventh millennium the world will not yet be renewed, and the righteous [will exist] as they did during [the era of] the resurrection, except that God, blessed is He, will make them wings.... During the renewal, God, blessed is He, will completely remake the world.

In the world that exists today, we see that the body is completely dominant [over the soul], as a man rules his household, because this alone is its [natural] habitat. However, during the seventh millennium, the righteous will be lifted beyond the earth [i.e., beyond their earthly needs]. The body will remain outside its natural sphere, like a man wandering from his home or a guest lodging for a night. Therefore, it will no longer retain its dominance....

Therefore, Chazal referred to the seventh millennium as "a day that is completely Shabbos, eternal rest" (based on *Tehillim* 92:1; see *Sanhedrin* 97a) — the body rests from all corporeal functions, which are [represented by] the weekdays. However, [during the seventh millennium] the body has still not abrogated its nature, because the creation has not been renewed. But from the renewal onward, which is [referred to as] "tomorrow to receive their reward" (based on *Devarim* 7:10; see *Eiruvin* 22a), there is no longer any need for the preeminence of the body, which was necessary only for service [of God] in its time. The body will become subordinate to the soul [to enable the body] to rejoice eternally in Heavenly good.

(Ramchal, *Da'as Tevunos* 92)

DANIEL: What will the world itself be like after the destruction?

RABBI COHEN: Unfortunately, this is where our inquiry must end. We have no idea what *Olam HaBa*, the renewed world, will be like. We do understand its purpose in the scheme of creation — it's the place where a person will enjoy the fruits of his labor in this world. But as far as physical details, we have no idea.

Rabbi Yaakov says: This world is like a corridor before the World to Come; prepare yourself in the corridor so you may enter the banquet hall.

(*Avos* 4:16)

We have mentioned that man is the creature that was created to cling to God. Man is placed between perfection and deficiency, with the capability of acquiring perfection.... Therefore, man was created with a good inclination and an evil inclination, with the choice of directing himself to whichever side he chooses....

God's goodness decreed that there be a [time] limit to the required effort of man to attain perfection. When his [period of] effort is complete, he attains perfection and revels in its enjoyment for all eternity. Therefore, God created two periods — one a time of labor and one a time of receiving reward....

Therefore, God created two worlds, this world and *Olam HaBa*. The environment and natural laws of this world are necessary for man during the period of labor, and the environment and laws of *Olam HaBa* are necessary for man during the period of receiving reward.

(Ramchal, *Derech Hashem* I:3:1–4)

In fact, we will not speak of [the seventh millennium and the renewal of the world]. We certainly know of the existence of those periods and their general character, and it is in this respect that we speak of the body and soul. But we cannot understand and know the [precise] details of those periods at all....

(Ramchal, *Da'as Tevunos* 94)

DANIEL: And *Olam HaBa* lasts forever?

RABBI COHEN: Yes, the reward of *Olam HaBa* is eternal. The righteous will forever continue the process of attaining perfection and becoming progressively closer to God.

Many of those who sleep in the dusty earth will awaken; these for everlasting life and those for shame, for everlasting abhorrence.

(*Daniel* 12:2; see also *Ramban, Sha'ar HaGemul* 346)

DANIEL: Okay, let me sum up the major points we've learned today.

We explained that during the era of the Moshiach there will be two separate resurrections of the dead. The first will happen soon after the arrival of the Moshiach, but only the righteous will rise at that time. A second resurrection will take place at the end of the era of the Moshiach. Everyone who ever lived will rise at that time to be judged by God. Then the world will go through a thousand-year period of destruction. Finally, the world will be renewed in its permanent state, that of *Olam HaBa*. The righteous will live there, enjoying the rewards they earned during a lifetime of service to God. At the same time, they will attain increasingly greater perfection and continue to become closer to God.

We also explained that, according to the majority opinion, our final state of existence will be with both body and soul, similar to the way we live today. Since the reward of *Olam HaBa* involves being close to God, a spiritual pleasure, it's obvious why we need our soul. But the body is also necessary — in the same way that the body served God, it also deserves to be rewarded. Also, since God desires that we retain this form, even the physical body contains deep secrets, many beyond our comprehension. Ultimately the soul will purify the body to the point that even the physical body will be able to experience the spiritual pleasure of closeness to God.

RABBI COHEN: Excellent! Now, if I'm not mistaken, we really have reached the end of your questions.

DANIEL: Yeah, I guess we have. But can I ask you just one more?

RABBI COHEN: Of course.

DANIEL: Well...not that I think you've been holding out on me or anything, but can't you at least give me a hint to when the Moshiach might arrive?

RABBI COHEN: I can tell you this much, my friend. It will be soon.

DANIEL: Hmm...

RABBI COHEN: I want you to keep one thing in mind. Now that you understand the principles of the era of the Moshiach, don't spend too much time thinking about these matters. Our job is to concentrate our thoughts and efforts on the truly important things: Torah, mitzvos, and *teshuvah*. The more we focus our efforts, the sooner the Moshiach will arrive. It's that simple. And if these learning sessions are the catalyst for even an ounce of change in the right direction, it will all have been worthwhile.

DANIEL: I really appreciate the time you've given me these last few weeks.

RABBI COHEN: You can believe me when I tell you that I gained at least as much as you. It's practically impossible to learn about these concepts and not be inspired to self-improvement. I pray that by the next time we meet, the Moshiach will have arrived — quickly and in our lifetime.

DANIEL: Amen!

Week 9

9/11 and beyond

Three months later, following the tragic events of September 11, 2001...

DANIEL: Hey, it's great bumping into you, Rabbi Cohen.

RABBI COHEN: How have you been doing?

DANIEL: Great. Actually, I've been meaning to call you. Do you have a few minutes to discuss our favorite topic?

RABBI COHEN: For you? Of course.

DANIEL: I've wanted to ask you about all of these great proofs I've seen about nine eleven and the redemption.

RABBI COHEN: Oh?

DANIEL: Yeah, this stuff is great. Isn't there a verse in *Tzefaniah* that talks about the Twin Towers? And aren't there verses that say the attacks on America are the start of the War of Gog U'Magog? And aren't there proofs that the Moshiach has to arrive within twenty-nine —

RABBI COHEN: Whoa, slow down, my friend. If you think I'm the one to discuss these proofs with, you're barking up the wrong tree.

DANIEL: I am? I mean, isn't this your specialty?

RABBI COHEN: I'll admit that I studied the concepts of the era of the

Moshiach, just as you and I did together. But as far as supposed, specific proofs — "this verse refers to this event" and "this *Zohar* means that the Moshiach will arrive by such-and-such a date" — I make every effort to stay away from those.

DANIEL: Stay away? But why? I don't understand.

RABBI COHEN: Listen closely, because the point I'm going to make is subtle. I want you to understand that your heart is in the right place. Any rational person cannot help but be awed and frightened by the cataclysmic events that are taking place around us. Also, you clearly realize that these events require a response. We cannot act as if nothing has occurred. It's vital that we react. The question is, what's the appropriate response?

The *gedolim* tell us that in these times, as in any time of trouble, our obligation is to focus on learning Torah and doing *teshuvah*. The problem with your "proofs" is that they have a tendency to distract a person from their primary obligations. When a person looks at the unfolding events through the prism of these "proofs," he tends to see them as a part of a predetermined plan of which we have little part.

DANIEL: But isn't it true? Didn't you say yourself that this is *ikvesa d'Meshicha* (week 5)?

RABBI COHEN: It's a question of emphasis. Do we say the Twin Towers were attacked, but it was predicted in *Tzefaniah* and therefore just part of the process? Or do we say that the Twin Towers were attacked, and therefore we had better start taking our own responsibilities seriously?

Looking into the *Zohar* and *midrashim* is enticing because they offer a possible glimpse into the process of redemption. They make

a person feel good because he thinks he understands the tumultu-
ous events. He is no longer confused or frightened, because this is,
after all, just part of *ikvesa d'Meshicha*. And he quickly becomes dis-
tracted from his own obligations — Torah study, *teshuvah*, and
prayer.

DANIEL: So what you're saying is that it really makes no difference
whether the verse in *Tzefaniah* refers to the destruction of the Twin
Towers or not. The important thing is that I concentrate on my
personal obligations.

RABBI COHEN: You should know that after the Yom Kippur War,
when thousands of Jews were killed, a similar phenomenon took
place. People began talking about the redemption and the various
hints and proofs that the arrival of the Moshiach was imminent.

The great *rosh yeshivah* and leader of the generation, Rav Eliezer
Menachem Mann Shach, *zt"l*, in a public speech made a point similar
to the one we just discussed. All the hints and proofs divert a person's
attention from their real obligations. Of course we must react — but
only by strengthening our Torah learning, *teshuvah,* and prayer.

DANIEL: I see what you mean. They must have really felt the end
was near, just like they felt during the Holocaust.

RABBI COHEN: But ultimately the hints and proofs came to nothing.
The only thing that endures is the change we make in ourselves
and the Torah we learn.

DANIEL: So why did we learn about the Moshiach in the first place?
Was it all a waste of time?

RABBI COHEN: Of course not. First of all, the learning itself is Torah,
one of the greatest mitzvos that exists. It's also vital for us to understand the underlying ideas of the era of the Moshiach, just as we

must try to understand all the mitzvos of the Torah to the best of our ability. After all, the Moshiach and the resurrection are principles of the Jewish faith. But if you remember our learning sessions, you'll realize that we always stuck to the ideas rather than their real-life counterparts. We discussed the Moshiach, but we never theorized who he might be. We talked about Gog U'Magog, but we never suggested which modern-day nation it might represent.

DANIEL: And we discussed the rules that govern the arrival of the Moshiach, but we never actually gave a date.

RABBI COHEN: Exactly. The truth is that studying about the era of the Moshiach can be very inspiring. But that inspiration should drive you to self-improvement, not to sitting around pondering hints and dates all day. Of course, I don't mean that looking at the hints and proofs is prohibited; occasionally, they also have the power to inspire. It's all a question of emphasis.

DANIEL: As usual, you've set me straight. Since I have you here, though, do you mind if I ask you one last question?

RABBI COHEN: Go ahead.

DANIEL: Well, I really wanted to ask you this question the last time we learned together, but I wasn't sure if I should. But now with all this stuff going on...I just have to hear your answer.

Why do you think the Moshiach hasn't arrived yet? The Inquisition, World War II, the Yom Kippur War, the al-Aqsa intifada, the Twin Towers — the Jewish people have suffered so much. What do you think is keeping the Moshiach from coming?

RABBI COHEN: That's an important question, and I'm glad you asked it. Obviously, only God knows the true answer. But let me ask you a question in return. Do you really want the Moshiach to come?

DANIEL: Of course I do.

RABBI COHEN: And you're ready for his arrival? All of your spiritual accounts are in order?

DANIEL: Well, sort of. I learn, I'm trying to work on myself, but...you know how hard it can be and...

RABBI COHEN: And?

DANIEL: All right, I admit it. I do want him to come pretty soon. But I'm not quite ready. There's still so many Gemaras I haven't learned, still so much *teshuvah* to do.

RABBI COHEN: So you want him to come, just not now.

DANIEL: Right. Wait...I mean, no. Hey, you tricked me!

RABBI COHEN: Did I? The truth is that many people feel the same way. Of course we want the Moshiach to arrive, but there are so many things we want to accomplish first. I'm not even talking about poor excuses, like wanting to finish the payments on your car or to conclude a big deal at work. I'm talking about the good reasons, the religious ones. Have I done enough *teshuvah*? Have I learned enough Torah? Am I really ready for his arrival?

> I sought and examined with all my heart to understand the reason for the lengthiness of this exile. I've found that in these generations there is much Torah in Yisrael. Much of the nation occupies itself in the study of Mishnah, Gemara, *poskim*, and the writings of Kabbalah, yet the redeemer has not arrived in Zion. Many people in these generations have prayed with all

their strength and fortitude. They cry, yet [their prayers] are not answered. Many people are occupied with such a multitude of mitzvos that they are filled with mitzvos like a pomegranate. Despite all this, the redemption does not arrive.... Therefore, I said to myself that it must be that there is some fault that stands against [these virtues].... Although we constantly discuss the coming of the Moshiach, it is hollow talk.... A person's true desire is to finish the building he is erecting, which will take years to complete, or to conclude the business deal for which he has lobbied the authorities or the kingdom for four or five years.

(Sefer HaBris 1:9:16; see also Mabit, Beis Elokim, Sha'ar HaTefillah 17)

DANIEL: But isn't there something to that train of thought? If he does arrive today, I would definitely be caught unprepared. So wouldn't it be better, for myself at least, if he delayed just a bit?

RABBI COHEN: Of course not. First, the rectification of the creation and the ultimate good that will take place during the messianic process vastly outweigh your personal concerns. But you also have to realize that, no matter what level you've attained, you'll always feel a desire to reach a higher level of spirituality, to go just a bit further, before the Moshiach arrives. So it's really a pointless line of reasoning. No matter who you are — and what you've achieved — you have to hope and pray with all your might for the arrival of the Moshiach.

DANIEL: I understand. Thanks for your time, Rabbi Cohen.

RABBI COHEN: No problem. Who knows? Maybe we'll find the time to learn about other subjects in the not-too-distant future.

DANIEL: That would be great. Take care.

RABBI COHEN: Take care, Daniel. Until next time.

Rabbi Cohen's Notes

On the eleventh day of Nissan 5762, I finished transcribing the discussions that took place between Daniel and me concerning the Moshiach and the World to Come. As I held the manuscript in my hands, I realized that someday it might form the basis for a book on the subject. However, because of time and other limitations, there were a few subjects we did not cover in as much depth as I would have wished. I have recorded these notes with the hope that I will find a way to work the changes into the main text.

1. This does not mean, however, that the Moshiach is incapable of fighting the battles single-handedly or that it is illogical to suggest. In fact, as the Sages tell us, this is precisely the way Avraham Avinu fought when rescuing Lot from captivity by the four kings (see *Bereishis* 14:12). However, the verses seem to suggest that the Moshiach will not engage in battle at all.

> One time the Jews wanted to send a gift to the House of Caesar. They said, "Nachum Ish Gam Zu should go, for he is used to [having] miracles [performed on his behalf]." They sent him with a chest filled with precious stones and pearls.

He went [on the journey] and spent a night in a certain residence [in Rome]. At night the residents took his chest. [They emptied the jewels] and filled it with dirt. When he arrived, they untied the chest and saw it was filled with dirt.

The emperor wanted to kill [the entire Jewish nation]. He said, "The Jews are mocking me!"

Nachum Ish Gam Zu said, "This, too, is for the best."

Eliyahu came and appeared as a Roman. He said to [the caesar], "Maybe this dirt comes from the dirt of their father Avraham. When he would throw dirt [at his enemies], it turned into swords; straw, and it turned into arrows, as it says, 'He made his sword like dirt, his bow like windblown straw' (*Yeshayah* 41:2)."

There was one country [the Romans] could not conquer. They tested some [of the dirt, and it turned into swords and arrows], and they conquered it. The Romans went into their treasure vault and filled [Nachum Ish Gam Zu's] chest with precious stones and pearls and sent him off with great honor.

(*Ta'anis* 21a)

2. See week 7 for further discussion on the War of Gog U'Magog.

3. As was obvious from our discussion, the Moshiach will be a normal human being, physiologically and otherwise, born of a mother and father like other men.

[The Moshiach] will be absolutely mortal, born of the union of a man and a woman like myself.

(Ramban, *Sefer HaVikuach* 88)

So Moshiach the king will be like one of us and will be so in every aspect, with respect to his mother and with respect to his father. He will also be among the people in exile, suffering the afflictions of the exile as the rest of his brethren....

(Abarbanel, *Yeshuos Meshicho* 3:3)

4. We established that there is a basic difference between prophecy and the attribute of *morach vada'in*. A potential Moshiach must manifest the trait of *morach vada'in* immediately, while it is possible that the Moshiach will become a prophet only over time. We did not, however, discuss the reason for this difference.

The answer, related to me by one of the giants of our generation, is that *morach vada'in* is a trait connected to the world as it exists today, while prophecy does not exist in our world. It is possible for anyone to be *morach vada'in* even nowadays, and there have been people who possessed the trait. The *Zohar* relates that a certain child once knew that Rabbi Yitzchak and Rabbi Yehudah had not said *Krias Shema*. When they asked how he knew, the child answered, "By the smell of your clothes" (*Zohar, Balak*, p. 186 [Vilna ed.]). Rabbi Chaim Vital wrote about the Ari HaKadosh that he could recognize the soul of a person by the "smell" of his clothes, similarly to the child mentioned in the *Zohar*.

Prophecy, however, disappeared after the time of the Men of the Great Assembly. The Sages tell us that there were people since then who deserved to receive prophecy, but did not, because their generation was unworthy.

It is clear from many verses that the Moshiach will possess every good character trait possible to attain. He will be righteous, wise, and generous. Since today it is also possible to possess the trait of *morach vada'in*, he must have it from the outset. But he will not necessarily attain prophecy immediately since it is temporarily unattainable in this world. Ultimately, the Moshiach will become a great prophet, second only to Moshe Rabbeinu.

5. For additional perspectives on the question of who killed Bar

Kochva, see Rambam, *Hilchos Melachim* 11:2; *Kessef Mishnah*, ad. loc.; *Lechem Mishneh*, ad. loc.; *Sanhedrin* 93b; and *Yad Ramah*, ad. loc.

6. Besides Yeshu and Bar Kochva, Shabbsai Tzvi is probably the most famous of the false messiahs in Jewish history. Shabbsai Tzvi, who lived in the seventeenth century, studied Kabbalah and practiced asceticism from a relatively young age. Ordained as a Sefardic rabbi before his twentieth birthday, he was both intelligent and diligent and was apparently well regarded in his community.

Later in life, however, he was affected by an illness akin to manic-depressive psychosis. He began to behave strangely and experience messianic delusions. While some Jewish communities drove him from their midst, others became convinced that his behavior was a sign of holiness and prophecy. In 1665, he publicly declared himself the Moshiach. Yet he continued his deviant behavior, eating non-kosher foods and violating other basic Torah laws.

Ultimately he was brought before the sultan of Turkey. Faced with the choice of converting to Islam or death, Shabbsai Tzvi chose apostasy. A small group persisted in believing that he was the Moshiach, but the overwhelming majority realized the charade was over.

7. As we said in the main text, according to the Rambam, belief in the coming of the Moshiach is one of the thirteen basic tenets of Judaism. Accordingly, a person who denies this principle (or any of the other twelve) is considered an apostate.

> And if a person doubts any of these principles, he is removed from the community and is a heretic....
>
> (Rambam, *Peirush HaMishnayos, Sanhedrin, Chelek*)

However, the Ba'al Halkarim argued that although the concept of the Moshiach is certainly true, and to disbelieve is a transgression, it is not considered a principle on which the entire Torah is dependent.

> Without a doubt Rabbi Hillel did not believe in the coming of the Moshiach at all. Nevertheless, he was not counted among the heretics, because the coming of the Moshiach is not [among the three most basic] tenets of the Torah of Moshe as the Rambam, *z"l*, wrote.... Rabbi Hillel was a transgressor because he did not believe in the coming of the redeemer, yet he was not a heretic. This is also the opinion of the later authorities....
>
> *(Sefer HaIkarim* 1:1)

Even the Rambam agrees that only belief in the general principle is a basic tenet of Judaism. Specific details, such as whether or not the arrival of Eliyahu HaNavi will proceed the arrival of the Moshiach or the manner in which the Moshiach will arrive, are not included in the tenet. Therefore a person who believes in the coming of the Moshiach yet does not believe one of these details is not considered an apostate.

> Nevertheless, neither the order of these events nor their specific details are principles of faith.
>
> (Rambam, *Hilchos Melachim* 12:2)

It is also worthy to note that although the Ba'al HaIkarim argued with the Rambam, the opinion of the Rambam has become accepted among the Jewish people.

8. While the Rambam states clearly that a person must await the arrival of the Moshiach, there are clearly additional criteria relevant to his arrival. For example, the Sages say that the Moshiach will not arrive on an *erev Shabbos* or *erev yom tov*. Also, the coming

of the Moshiach will be preceded by the arrival of Eliyahu HaNavi. Does this mean that on *erev Shabbos* or as long as Eliyahu has not appeared, I am free of the obligation to await the Moshiach?

> [If someone declares,] "I will be a *nazir* on the day that the son of David arrives," he is permitted to drink wine on Shabbos and *yom tov* [because we know that the Moshiach will not arrive on those days].
>
> (*Eiruvin* 43a)

> There [in the case of the Moshiach] it is different [from the case of Eliyahu HaNavi] because the verse says, "Behold, I will send you Eliyahu HaNavi [before the coming of the great and awesome day of God]" (*Malachi* 3:23), and [since] Eliyahu did not come the previous day [on *erev Shabbos* or *erev yom tov*, we know that the Moshiach will not arrive on Shabbos or *yom tov* itself].
>
> (Ibid. 43b)

The obligation to hope for the imminent arrival of the Moshiach is independent of our knowledge of the details of his arrival, even those that seem to indicate a delay. The Moshiach himself will resolve any apparent contradictions. A group of students once asked the Brisker Rav how we can truthfully await the coming of the Moshiach, since Eliyahu HaNavi still has yet to arrive. The Brisker Rav answered that when he arrives the Moshiach will answer the question of how he could arrive before Eliyahu.

> The obligation of our belief is not connected at all to the comprehension of those statements [of the Sages]. Even if we do not understand how it is possible, it will all be understood when the Moshiach arrives and reveals the hidden things. For us, our entire duty and obligation is to believe and to await his arrival at each and every moment.
>
> If a person does not await his arrival, he probably believes

in the general idea that the Moshiach will arrive someday, but he does not believe that he might arrive at any moment. He establishes times when [he feels] the Moshiach might arrive and conditions without which he cannot come. He decides that as long as [the Jewish nation] has not done *teshuvah*, or as long as the generation is not "entirely deserving or entirely undeserving," or as long as he has yet to see Eliyahu HaNavi with his own eyes, or as long as he does not witness the fulfillment of all the signs of the footsteps of the Moshiach, and so on, it is impossible for the Moshiach to come. Subsequently he does not await his arrival at each and every moment, but rather waits for him to come after the fulfillment of all the conditions and terms that he established according to the simple meaning of *midrashim* and the words of the Sages. He does not know the most basic idea, that the Moshiach will explain all the *midrashim* when he arrives....

(*Toras Zev*, p. 181, quoted in *Otzros Acharis HaYamim*, ch. 1)

9. The Maharal also explains at length that the covenant between God and the Jewish nation is not dependent on, or bound by, any condition at all. Even if we fail to perform His will, God will still fulfill His promises through us.

It is certain that the covenant [God] made with Avraham has not been canceled, because the covenant was never given a limitation or end. Rather, it is called "an eternal covenant." Therefore, why should the covenant be nullified for his unborn descendants simply because one or two past generations sinned? Therefore, the verse says, "Not with you alone do I seal this covenant and this oath, but with whoever is here [standing with us today before Hashem our God, and with whoever is not here with us today]" (*Devarim* 29:13–14).

(Maharal, *Netzach Yisrael* 11, s.v. "*u'bishemos rabbah*")

155

10. While it's true that the Sages clearly had a negative opinion regarding those who tried to calculate the date of the Moshiach's arrival, we find many (Rav Sa'adyah Gaon, the Ramban, and many *Acharonim*) who did attempt to calculate the date. How could they ignore the warnings of the Sages? I have located at least four answers to this question.

First, the Abarbanel answers that the entire prohibition against calculating the date is only if one does so by means of astrology. Calculations using verses from Tanach are permitted.

> But the Sages did not, in their words, denigrate a person who investigates and understands the date through the words of the prophets and *ruach hakodesh*. This was always their rule, to give signs and wonders [describing] the generation in which the son of David will arrive.... This was the opinion of the later Sages — the *Gaon* we mentioned, Rashi, Rabbi Avraham ben Rabbi Chiya, the Ramban, and others.
>
> (Abarbanel, *Ma'ayenei HaYeshua* 1:2)

The second answer can be found in the writings of the Ramban. He explains that only early generations (relative to the Ramban, who lived in the 1200s) were prohibited to calculate the date. Since the *Tannaim* and *Amoraim* knew that the date was still far off, they didn't want this revealed to the general populace lest they lose hope in the coming of the Moshiach. Later generations, however, are permitted to calculate the date.

> Before we open our lips to discuss the subject of the final date, we must rescue ourselves from what Chazal said: "May the essence of those who calculate dates [of the end of the exile] suffer agony!" I say their intention regarding this is what we said [previously], that there were those among Chazal who knew that the date was long after their time, as they said to Rabbi Akiva,

"Grass will grow on your cheek, and still the Moshiach will not have arrived" (*Pesikta Rabbasi* 2:5). They did not wish this revealed to the general populace lest it weaken their hope. And now these factors are canceled, since we are in the final days....

(Ramban, *Sefer HaGeulah* 4)

The Rambam mentions a third answer. As we discuss shortly in the main text, the entire prohibition was enacted to prevent people from losing faith if the date passes without the arrival of the Moshiach. During the time of the *Geonim*, however, Rav Sa'adyah Gaon found that due to the vicissitudes of the exile the people were disheartened and began to lose faith. By gathering many people to calculate the date, Rav Sa'adyah gave the Jewish people an infusion of faith, renewing their interest and hope in the Moshiach. In such a case, calculating the date is permitted.

We will rescue Rav Sa'adyah, z"l, and say that the only reason he did this — despite his opinion that it was [usually] prohibited — was because the people of his generation had many doubts in their faith...and he saw, as part of his efforts, to gather a multitude of people to calculate the date to strengthen their hope in the truth. [Rav Sa'adyah's] every action was for the sake of Heaven.

(Rambam, *Iggeres Teiman* 3)

Finally, both the Ramban and the Maharal explain that none of the Sages meant that a given time was positively the date of the Moshiach's arrival. Rather, the suggested dates were *possible* times of the arrival. This final answer also works in conjunction with the first three.

Because our words on the date are words of possibility...for we are not prophets to make a [definite] statement about the secrets of God.

(Ramban, *Sefer HaGeulah* 4)

As we explained in the main text, however, the date will never be known for certain. Therefore, a person must remain wary of the reason the Sages prohibited calculations in the first place. Additionally, since the question of calculating dates is halachic in nature, the above sources could not be taken as a *heter*, allowance, without express approval of a *posek*.

11. In the main text, we explained that there are two possibilities for the arrival of the Moshiach — voluntary *teshuvah* or the set time for his arrival. However, there are many sources that indicate that ultimately the Jewish people will do *teshuvah* either way. This seems to contradict the *midrash* we quoted, which stated that the Moshiach will arrive regardless of our actions; according to that, *teshuvah* is not an absolute necessity.

> Rabbi Eliezer says: If the Jewish people repent, they will be redeemed, and if not, they will not be redeemed. Rabbi Yehoshua said to him: If they do not repent, they will not be redeemed? Rather, the Holy One, blessed is He, will appoint over them a king whose decrees will be as harsh as [those of] Haman, and the Jewish people will repent....
>
> (*Sanhedrin* 97b)

> Rather, we have received a tradition from the prophets that troubles and pressure will assail us, which will cause us to choose to return [to God] and therefore be worthy of redemption. This is the [meaning of the] statement of our predecessors: if the Jewish people repent, they will be redeemed, and if not, the Holy One, blessed is He, will appoint over them a king whose decrees will be as harsh as [those of] Haman, and they will repent and be redeemed (based on *Sanhedrin* 97b).
>
> (Rav Sa'adyah Gaon, *Emunos V'Deos* 8:5)

Yisrael will not be redeemed without *teshuvah*, and the Torah has already assured us that Yisrael will ultimately do *teshuvah* at the end of their exile.

(Rambam, *Hilchos Teshuvah* 7:5)

The answer, related to me by one of the giants of this generation, is that without a doubt the Jewish people must do *teshuvah* before the Moshiach arrives. If we are not willing to do *teshuvah* of our own accord, God will force the Jewish nation to do *teshuvah*, as it says in the *gemara* quoted.

When the Sages said there are two possible times for the arrival of the Moshiach, one if we do *teshuvah* and one regardless, they meant this: If we do *teshuvah* of our own accord, the Moshiach will come immediately. If, however, we do not do *teshuvah* of our own accord, the Moshiach will arrive at the preset time. However, before that time God will arrange events that will cause the Jewish nation to do *teshuvah*.

Thus, in the main text, I was careful to refer to the Jewish nation doing *teshuvah* willingly as opposed to being forced to repent, because either way they will do *teshuvah*. According to one *midrash*, Eliyahu HaNavi will be the final catalyst that will inspire the Jewish people to do *teshuvah*.

Rabbi Yehudah says: If the people of Israel do not repent, they will not be redeemed. And they will repent only amid pain, wandering, and lack of sustenance. They will not repent until Eliyahu arrives, as it says, "Behold, I will send you Eliyahu HaNavi" (*Malachi* 3:23–24), which is followed by "And he will turn back [to God] the hearts of the fathers with the sons."

(*Yalkut Shimoni, Malachi* 595)

12. On the basis of my description, Daniel naturally assumed that our generation is the era preceding the Moshiach. The question

might be asked, why does our generation in particular seem to match? After all, many *Acharonim* and even *Rishonim* stated explicitly that their generation seemed to match the prerequisite signs. However, it is clear that in certain respects our generation is truly unique. For example, there has always been a small percentage of assimilated Jews. Yet it has only been since the Enlightenment of the eighteenth century, and even more so since the destruction of European Jewry during the Second World War, that assimilation has reached the monstrous proportions that match the descriptions of the Sages, as described in the sources in the main text.

Similarly, the Sages said that preceding the arrival of the Moshiach the Land of Israel will once again bloom fully. As recently as seventy years ago, Israel was a desolate land of malaria-infested swamplands and barren desert.

> And why did they establish that we say [the blessing of] the ingathering of the exiles after the blessing of the years? For it is written, "You, mountains of Israel, will shoot forth your branches and produce your fruit for My people, Israel, for they are close to returning" (*Yechezkel* 36:8).
>
> (*Megillah* 17b)

> Rabbi Abba said: There is no clearer indication of the [final] date than this, as it says, "You, mountains of Israel, will shoot forth your branches and produce your fruit for My people, Israel..." (*Yechezkel* 36:8).
>
> (*Sanhedrin* 98a)

Also, the Sages said that the arrival of the Moshiach will be preceded by wars between the nations of the world. True, there has rarely, if ever, been a time of complete peace on earth. However, the First and Second World Wars, by name and by magnitude, are certainly recognized as having been greater than previous wars.

Note the language of the *Yalkut Shimoni* below: "all the nations of the world." A close investigation will show that these, and many other signs, have occurred only quite recently.

> Rabbi Eliezer bar Avina said: If you see kingdoms quarreling with one another, await the footsteps of the Moshiach.
>
> (*Midrash Rabbah, Bereishis* 42:4)

> Rabbi Yitzchak said: In the year in which Moshiach the king will be revealed, all the kingdoms of the world will quarrel with each other.... And all the nations of the world will tremble and be frightened and fall on their faces, and they will be seized by pains like birth pangs. And Israel will tremble and be frightened and say, "To where should we come and go?"
>
> (*Yalkut Shimoni, Yeshayah* 499)

See also *Pirkei D'Rabbi Eliezer* 30 and 32 for a description of the actions of *bnei Yishmael*, the descendants of Yishmael, in the final days.

13. As we saw in note 11, *teshuvah* is a prerequisite for the redemption. Therefore, the connection is even stronger — since we must do *teshuvah*, we must experience the birth pangs of the Moshiach. However, if the Jewish people repent of their own initiative, they will not necessarily have to experience the birth pangs of the Moshiach at all.

Along these lines, there is yet another relationship between repentance and the birth pangs of the Moshiach. Not only will the birth pangs be a catalyst for repentance, but they will also take the place of repentance. Meaning, the birth pangs will act to purify the Jewish people in the same way that repentance and Torah study does. This is true of afflictions in general and is mentioned in the sources specifically in connection with the birth pangs of the Moshiach.

> For by means of the afflictions, their souls will be cleansed, and

the sparks of holiness will be purified in the same way that they are purified by means of the Torah, except that one is pleasant work, while the other is unpleasant work.

(Ohr HaChaim, Bereishis 49:11)

"Rabbi Yehoshua ben Levi said: It is enough that the mourner remain in mourning" — meaning, it is enough for Yisrael, who waits and mourns over their exile. Even without *teshuvah*, it is only just that they be redeemed, for they are atoned by their exile.

(Yad Ramah, Sanhedrin 97b, s.v. "amar Rav")

See also *Kesubos* 112b, s.v. "*Rabbi Zeira amar,*" for an additional insight into the reasons for the birth pangs of the Moshiach.

14. This is analogous to what occurred at the end of the Babylonian exile. Those who were living peacefully and comfortably in Bavel refused to return to Eretz Yisrael with Ezra the scribe. Only the poor and those with no stake in Bavel went with him.

[Ezra] could not find [Kohanim and Levi'im] fit for service [in the Beis HaMikdash among those who ascended with him to Eretz Yisrael], for they were dwelling peacefully in Bavel. Those who ascended to Yerushalayim were poor, burdened with labor and fearful of their surroundings.

(Rashi, Kiddushin 69b, s.v. "v'avinah b'am")

Only a small number ascended with Ezra. The *gedolim*, the wise men, and the nobility of Israel remained in Bavel.

(Sefer HaIkarim 3:22)

15. This idea is true of the generation in which the Moshiach arrives and also of the level of the Jewish people. The Jewish nation itself will be on the lowest level possible before the advent of the redemption in order that the redemption will have the greatest

impact on them. This is the meaning of the following *midrash*:

> Israel said before the Holy One, blessed is He, "Master of the world, when will You redeem us?" God answered, "When you descend to the lowest level, I will redeem you," as it says, "The children of Yehudah and the children of Israel will be assembled together, and they will appoint one head for themselves and ascend from the land" (*Hoshea* 2:2). And it says, "For our soul is prostrate to the dust" (*Tehillim* 44:26). What is written afterward? "Arise! Assist us!" God said, "Everything is [dependent] on you, like a rose that blossoms with its core upraised. So too, when you do *teshuvah* like a rose, with your hearts directed toward [God] above, I will redeem you," as it says, "I will be to Israel like the dew" (*Hoshea* 14:6). When [will God soothe Israel like dew]? When "he will blossom like a rose" (ibid.).
>
> (Yalkut Shimoni, Hoshea 533)

16. This is the second example of the divine guidance that will exist as the world is being prepared for redemption and ultimate perfection. Previously (week 3) we noted that false messiahs existed for the sole purpose of spreading the ideas of the Messiah and redemption. Here we see that God is guiding the entire course of history to ensure that the arrival of the Moshiach be experienced from a state of contrast. In fact, the exile itself is an aspect of this underlying plan. The Maharsha explains that since the Jewish nation was scattered across the globe, the world has become aware of its beliefs and teachings. As we saw, ultimately even the gentile nations will devote their attention to understanding and knowing God.

> "For I have scattered you like the four directions of the heavens" (*Zechariah* 2:10). What does this verse mean? If you say [it means] God scattered them *to* the four directions, [instead of] "like the four directions" it should have said "to the four

directions." Rather, just as it is impossible for the world [to survive] without wind, so too it is impossible for the world [to survive] without Israel. [Thus they are likened to the four winds.]

(*Avodah Zarah* 10b)

Because He spread and scattered them to the four directions, their beliefs and their Torah have become publicized to the entire world, and that is what sustains the world.

(*Maharsha*, ad. loc.)

Even a cursory glance at modern American culture shows the great surge of interest in traditional Orthodox Jewry. Popular novels, major motion pictures, and even the candidacy of Senator Joseph Lieberman in the presidential race of 2000 have all served to spread knowledge of Torah values far and wide. On the success of *To Kindle a Soul* by Lawrence Kelemen, *Jerusalem Post* reporter Gail Lichtman wrote the following:

Some even muse about the possibility of Orthodox Judaism becoming an "in" philosophy, a kind of ancient wisdom for modern minds, resembling the way Eastern religions were revered in the twentieth.... *To Kindle a Soul* is only one of a number of Jewish books which have broken through from the Jewish to the larger U.S. market in the last few years.... "The mainstream book companies and bookstores are buying Jewish books because they think they can sell them," [Rabbi David] Aaron, [dean and founder of Isralight, an international Jewish education organization] says. "There is a trend now on the part of non-Jews to read these books, reflecting a greater interest by non-Jews in learning about Judaism."

("A Great Awakening," *Jerusalem Post*, October 10, 2001)

17. We know little of the exact events surrounding the arrival of the Moshiach. This is especially true in the light of the fact that the

details of the arrival may differ according to the manner in which the redemption takes place, as it says in the main text (week 4). However, we do know that the revelation of the Moshiach will take place in Eretz Yisrael.

> Nevertheless, how he will arise and where he will arise — he will arise specifically in Eretz Yisrael. And there he will begin to be revealed, as the prophet says, "Suddenly the Master whom you seek will come to His Sanctuary" (*Malachi* 3:1).
>
> (Rambam, *Iggeres Teiman* 4)

Second, the arrival of the Moshiach will occur in a sudden manner. In the following verse, "the Master" refers to the Moshiach, while "the messenger of the covenant" refers to Eliyahu HaNavi.

> "Behold, I am sending My messenger, and he will clear a path before Me; suddenly the Master whom you seek will come to His Sanctuary, and the messenger of the covenant whom you desire, behold, he comes," says God, Master of legions.
>
> (*Malachi* 3:1)

> Since the [final date of the] end was not revealed and was not clarified in the book of *Daniel*, the verse says that he will come suddenly. No one knows the day of his arrival before he comes, as it says, "Because the matters are obscured and sealed until the time of the end" (*Daniel* 12:9).
>
> (*Radak, Malachi* 3:1)

> Three things arrive unexpectedly: the Moshiach, a found object, and a scorpion.
>
> (*Sanhedrin* 97a)

This is more than just a theoretical principle; it is the actual basis for halachic rulings. According to the Gemara, if a person vows he will become a *nazir* on the day the Moshiach arrives, he is prohibited from ever drinking wine (with the exception of Shabbos and *yom tov*, days on which the Sages say the Moshiach will not arrive). The vow would take effect retroactively to the beginning of the day of the Moshiach's arrival. Therefore he must never drink wine for fear the Moshiach might arrive at any moment, possibly near the end of the day.

> [If someone declares] "I am a *nazir* on the day the son of David arrives," he is permitted to drink wine on Shabbos and *yom tov* and is prohibited from drinking wine on weekdays.
>
> (*Eiruvin* 43a)

> "And he is prohibited [from drinking wine] on weekdays" — because [the Moshiach] might arrive.
>
> (*Rashi*, ad. loc.)

18. In fact, it is clear from the words of the Ramban that people will no longer possess free will during the time of the Moshiach. Unfortunately, beyond the quoted sources, there is little discussion of the nature of free will during the era of the Moshiach in the writings of the *Rishonim* and *Acharonim*.

It seems that, according to the Rambam, people will retain their free will. He writes, quoting Shmuel, that there is no difference between this world and the time of the Moshiach with the exception that we will no longer be oppressed by hostile nations (but see *Lechem Mishneh, Hilchos Teshuvah* 8:7).

However, there is much room for doubt that this was the Rambam's intention. The Rambam writes in *Hilchos Teshuvah* that the verse "I will remove your heart of stone [i.e., the evil inclination] from your flesh and give you a heart of flesh" (*Yechezkel* 36:26) applies to the time of the Moshiach. This seems to indicate that there will be no free will during the era of the Moshiach.

Rav Yehudah Chayoun, in his work *Otzros Acharis HaYamim,* quotes HaRav Chaim Kanievsky, *shlita,* as having said that according to the Rambam there will be free will during the time of the Moshiach.

Yet it is clear that even if the Rambam holds that there will be free will during the era of the Moshiach, it will be to a lesser degree than it is today. The Ramban, Maharal, and Ramchal, on the other hand, are quite explicit on the matter. Therefore I stated in the main text that the power of the evil inclination will be reduced, which is true according to all opinions.

> In those days knowledge, wisdom, and truth will increase, as it says, "The earth will be as filled with knowledge of God [as water covering the seabed]" (*Yeshayah* 11:9)...and it says, "I will remove the heart of stone from your flesh [and give you a heart of flesh]" (*Yechezkel* 36:26).
>
> (Rambam, *Hilchos Teshuvah* 9:2)

> The Sages said: There is no difference between this world and the days of the Moshiach, except for the oppression by [enemy] nations.
>
> (Rambam, *Hilchos Melachim* 12:2; see also *Gra,* ad. loc.; *Otzros Acharis HaYamim,* ch. 10, n. 10)

19. See also *Avodah Zarah* 3b for additional insight into why converts will not be accepted during the time of the Moshiach.

20. The Rambam quoted in the main text states clearly that no facet of the Torah will ever change. However, the following sources seem to indicate that certain mitzvos will change during the time of the Moshiach.

> Rabbi Yochanan said: In the future, the [books of the] Prophets and Writings will be neglected, and the five books of the Torah will not be neglected.
>
> (*Yerushalmi, Megillah* 1:5)

In the future, during the days of the Moshiach, all the [books of the] Prophets and the Writings will be neglected, except the Scroll of Esther, which will endure as the five books of the Torah, and the halachos of the Oral Law, which will never be neglected.

(Rambam, *Hilchos Megillah* 2:18)

"...She [Esther] also prepared her table" (*Mishlei* 9:2) — meaning she prepared her table in this world and also in the World to Come. What "name of renown" (ibid.) did she acquire? That in the future all the festivals will be neglected, while the days of Purim will never be neglected. Rabbi Eliezer said: Yom Kippur will also never be neglected, as it says, "This shall be to you an eternal decree" (*Vayikra* 16:34).

(*Yalkut Shimoni, Mishlei* 944)

The Alshich gives a beautiful explanation of the idea behind some of the books of the Prophets and Writings being neglected. The Sages tell us that every single lesson contained in the Prophets and Writings is hinted at somewhere in the Torah itself. However, the Alshich explains, it takes fantastic wisdom and insight to recognize those hints. As the world exists today, that level of understanding is beyond our ability. Yet during the time of the Moshiach, when the world will be filled with wisdom, we will understand even subtle nuances of the Torah and have insight into each lesson it contains. At that time, people will no longer study the Prophets and the Writings, because they will already understand the lessons they offer from the Torah itself.

I saw what HaRav Moshe Alshich, *z"l*, wrote on this topic in his work on *Megillas Esther*. He explained things according to their simple meaning, so that the question of the Ra'avad is no longer difficult. [He explains that] there is no book [of Tanach] that does not contain a lesson. It is certainly true that there is no book of the Prophets and Writings that does not contain a lesson to teach us. Yet it is [also] true, according to what the Sages said, that there is nothing written in the Prophets and Writings that is not hinted at in the Torah [itself]. Therefore, all [of these lessons] of the Prophets and Writings are hinted at, but it requires great insight to derive these hints from the Torah.... All this applies nowadays. But in the future, about which it says, "And the world will be filled with wisdom"...people will no longer need to learn [the lessons of] one from the other, and they will know and understand everything from the Prophets and Writings that is hinted at in the Torah. They will no longer need [the Prophets and Writings] at all, and they will be completely neglected. We will know and learn everything from the Torah itself, which will never be neglected.

(Mareh HaPanim, Yerushalmi, Megillah 1:5)

The Abarbanel gives a fascinating explanation of why the Sages said some of the festivals will be neglected in the time of the Moshiach. He explains that most of the festivals are based, in part or wholly, on the redemption from Egypt, the greatest miraculous process ever witnessed by the Jewish nation. The future redemption, however, will be so much greater that people will no longer even discuss the first redemption. The miracles that took place during the redemption from Egypt will, in effect, become secondary to the miracles and wonders that will take place during the final redemption. This was stated explicitly by the prophet, as it says, " 'Therefore, behold, days are coming,' says God, 'when it will no longer be said, 'The Living God Who took the children of Israel out of the land of Egypt,' but rather, 'The Living God Who took the children of Israel out of the Land of the North and from all the lands where He had scattered them' " (*Yirmeyah* 16:14). Yet the performance of the mitzvos, such as taking a *lulav*, sitting in a sukkah, and eating matzah, will of course still remain in effect.

> What [the Sages] say, "All the festivals will be neglected except for Purim and Yom Kippur," does not mean neglecting the mitzvos of the festivals — neither the mitzvah of Pesach and the prohibition against *chametz* and the mitzvah of matzah on the festival of Pesach nor sitting in a sukkah nor taking a *lulav* on the festival of Sukkos and the rest of the mitzvos of the Torah. It is impossible that a change will take place in any of these, but the relative importance of commemorating [the origins of these mitzvos] will no longer be significant.
>
> The reason we make the festivals in commemoration of the redemption of Egypt and glorify them is because we have never experienced a greater miracle. Yet because the [final] redemption will be so much greater than the redemption from Egypt, people will no longer pay attention to the commemoration of the redemption from Egypt and the miracles and wonders that were performed as they left. For when they see the great wonders that God will perform in the days of the Moshiach, they will forget the earlier ones.
>
> (Abarbanel, *Yeshuos Meshicho* 4:4; see also Rashba, Responsa 1:93; Radbaz, Responsa 2:428)

21. It is somewhat difficult to present a coherent summary of the opinions that explain details of the war, but we do know the following: According to the majority opinion, the War of Gog U'Magog will occur either after or during the ingathering of the exiles. According to many opinions, Gog U'Magog is a collection of nations who will attack Eretz Yisrael with the intention of looting and destroying the Jewish people. The *Mahari Kra*, however, seems to say that they will not attack Eretz Yisrael to fight the Jewish people per se, but only to conquer the land. According to

both views, the army of Gog U'Magog is the sole army involved in the war.

The Abarbanel and the Malbim, however, offer a different interpretation — that the war will involve two armies. They explain that sometime before the war Eretz Yisrael will be conquered by Edom, the spiritual and cultural descendants of Rome. The Arab nations, Gog U'Magog among them, will then attempt to wrest control of Eretz Yisrael from Edom, and a war will ensue.

For additional insight into the reasons behind the War of Gog U'Magog, see *Zechariah* 12:2 and *Malbim*, ad. loc.; *Zechariah* 13:9 and *Rashi* and *Metzudas David*, ad. loc.; *Avodah Zarah* 3b, s.v. "*Rabbi Yosei omer le'asid lavo.*"

22. As mentioned in the main text, there are many sources that state explicitly that Eliyahu HaNavi's arrival will precede the Moshiach.

> One time our masters and the rest of the Sages were sitting in the *beis midrash* and arguing [about] Eliyahu's lineage. One said he descended from Rachel; another said he descended from Leah. While they were arguing with one another, I [Eliyahu] came and appeared before them and said, "My masters, I descend only from Rachel.... First I will arrive in Bavel, and afterward the son of David will arrive."
>
> *(Tanna D'Bei Eliyahu* 18:49, quoted in
> *Tosafos, Bava Metzia* 114b, s.v. *"mahu")*

> "How pleasant are the footsteps of the herald upon the mountains..." (*Yeshayah* 52:7). At the time when God redeems Israel, three days before the Moshiach arrives, Eliyahu will arrive....
>
> *(Pesikta Rabbasi,* quoted in *Otzros Acharis HaYamim,* ch. 6;
> see also *Eiruvin* 43a, s.v. *"hareini nazir b'yom sheben David ba")*

Yet according to the simple meaning of the Rambam's words in

Hilchos Melachim, the Sages disagreed on this matter. Some, says the Rambam, claim the Moshiach will arrive before Eliyahu.

> It seems from the simple meaning of the words of the prophets that the War of Gog U'Magog will occur at the beginning of the days of the Moshiach. Before the War of Gog U'Magog, a prophet [Eliyahu] will arise to straighten Yisrael and to prepare their hearts, as it says, "Behold, I will send you, Eliyahu the prophet [before the coming of the great and awesome day of God]" (*Malachi* 3:23).... And there is an opinion of the Sages that states that Eliyahu will come before the arrival of Moshiach the king.
>
> (Rambam, *Hilchos Melachim* 12:2)

However, according to the *Kreisi U'Pleisi* and others, the Rambam's source for this dissenting opinion is not precisely clear. There does not seem to be any record of such an opinion in the Gemara and Midrash. Therefore, the *Kreisi U'Pleisi* suggests that even according to the Rambam there is no disagreement among the Sages. Rather, the Rambam meant that there are two possible scenarios for the arrival of Eliyahu. If the Jewish people do *teshuvah* voluntarily and bring the redemption "early," the Moshiach will arrive immediately, and only afterward will Eliyahu arrive. If the redemption arrives on the final, set date of his arrival (see week 4), Eliyahu will precede the Moshiach.

To sum up, most sources indicate Eliyahu will arrive before the Moshiach, and according to the Rambam there is at most a disagreement on the matter. Therefore, in the main text I stated that according to the overwhelming majority Eliyahu will arrive before the Moshiach. See also *Tosafos Yom Tov, Sanhedrin* 1:3; *Chasam Sofer*, Responsa, vol. 10, 98, s.v. *"shani"*; *Kreisi U'Pleisi* 110, *Kuntres HaSofek*, s.v. *"amnam"*; *VaYoel Moshe, Ma'amar Shalosh Shavuos* 53, s.v. *"shuv ra'isi."*

23. The purpose of the resurrection according to the Rambam is not readily apparent. According to him, after the body dies the soul passes to *Olam HaBa*, its final, spiritual existence. The soul has already completed its journey and arrived at its resting place. So why must the soul return to the mundane, physical world?

The first answer is identical to the explanation of why, according to the Ramban, the body is necessary for eternal existence (see further in main text). Since the soul is rewarded for its actions in this world, the body must also be rewarded. Therefore, the body and soul will be rejoined, albeit temporarily, in order that the physical half can receive its due. Ultimately, however, the primary reward of *Olam HaBa* is meant for the soul alone. Therefore, the body will perish once more, according to the Rambam, and the soul will return to *Olam HaBa*, its permanent resting place.

> Despite the fact that the primary reward is for the soul alone, there is another, physical reward during the days of the Moshiach, when the completely righteous rise during the resurrection of the dead. [There are many purposes to this resurrection. First,] it will publicize the miracles of God and [increase] belief of Him in the world. Also, it will allow them to attain physical pleasure commensurate with or greater than the days of their suffering [while alive], according to divine wisdom. Finally, it will allow them to attain greater perfection than they had attained before. Because of external oppression and the exile, they were unable, while alive, to attain a level that befitted their uprightness.
>
> (*Sefer HaIkarim* 4:30; see also *Sanhedrin* 91a; Rabbeinu Bachyai, *Devarim* 30:15; Ramchal, *Da'as Tevunos* 68, all quoted earlier in the main text)

A second reason for the resurrection, according to the Rambam, is in order to give a person a second chance to acquire perfection. In fact, it is a greater opportunity than the first time the soul experienced life. During the person's first lifetime, the troubles and vicissitudes of the exile prevented him from channeling his energy into the service of God, so he could not attain his full measure of spiritual perfection. In the era of the Moshiach, however, the Jewish people will be free to serve God with peace of mind (see week 1). Therefore, they will reach greater spiritual heights than before.

> When a person is troubled with sickness, war, and hunger in this world, he [cannot] be occupied with wisdom and mitzvos, with which he merits life in the World to Come. For this reason, all of Yisrael, and their prophets and Sages, desired the era of the king Moshiach. We will be relieved from the wicked kingdom, which does not allow Yisrael to occupy themselves properly with Torah and mitzvos.
>
> (Rambam, *Hilchos Teshuvah* 9:1–2)

The *Ba'al HaIkarim* (*Sefer HaIkarim* 4:30, quoted above; see also Shelah, *Beis David*, pp.17–18) mentions a third reason for the resurrection of the dead according to the Rambam. Previously (see week 7) we discussed the underlying reason the War of Gog U'Magog will occur precisely at the height of the redemption. We explained that the miraculous events of the war will help to convince the world of God's existence and might. Similarly, the miraculous nature of the resurrection will add to the world's belief in the existence and greatness of God.

24. According to this opinion, when a person dies, his soul goes to *Olam HaNeshamos*, the World of Souls. There it exists until it will rejoin with the body at the time of the resurrection of the dead. In the World of Souls, the soul derives pleasure from its closeness to God, similar to the pleasure of *Olam HaBa*.

Since death has been decreed on man, as we explained, this combination [of body and soul] must be separated for a period of time, ultimately to be reunited. During this period of separation, there must be an appropriate place for the individual parts.

Since the body originated from the dust, it must return to its element and lose its form. This is what God [meant when He] said to Adam, "You are dust, and to dust you must return" (*Bereishis* 3:19). The worthy soul, however, need only wait until the process the body must go through — decay and decomposition — is complete. The body must remain in the earth for as long as necessary, then be rebuilt anew so that the soul can return. During this period, however, the soul also needs a place [to rest]. Therefore God prepared the World of Souls.

When a soul leaves its body, it enters this World of Souls and remains there at rest while the body experiences what it must. During this entire period, the soul is in a state of sublime delight, similar to that which it will experience later during the period of reward, as we explained above.

(Ramchal, *Derech Hashem* I:3:11)

25. The verse from *Bereishis* quoted in the main text seems to imply that Adam HaRishon would have died on the day he ate from the tree. Yet Adam lived for 930 years. The explanation is as follows: Based on a verse in *Tehillim*, Chazal learn that God's "days" last a thousand years. Therefore, Adam did in fact die within the first "day" that he ate from the tree.

Why did Adam live for only 930 years rather than a thousand? The Midrash answers that after the creation of the world, God gave Adam a glimpse of his future descendants. When Adam saw that King David was destined to die at birth, Adam offered to give David a portion of his own life essence. Therefore, David lived for seventy years, which were taken from Adam's lifespan.

> For a thousand years in Your eyes are like a yesterday that has already passed....
>
> (*Tehillim* 90:4)

> God showed Adam a vision of all the future generations. He showed him David, who was destined to live for three hours. He said, "Master of the universe, is there no remedy for this [infant]?" God answered, "This is what I preordained." Adam said, "How many years will I live?" God answered, "One thousand years." Adam said, "Does the concept of giving a [spiritual] gift exist in Heaven?" God answered, "Yes." Adam said, "Seventy years of my life should be added to his fate." What did Adam do? He brought parchment and wrote a gift contract. God, blessed is He, the angel Matatron, and Adam signed the contract.
>
> (*Yalkut Shimoni, Bereishis* 41)

26. In the main text, we discussed how God will use the *luz*, also referred to as the *"naschui,"* to resurrect the dead. Yet another question must be addressed. What makes the *luz* special? Why is the *luz* immune to the decomposition that affects the rest of the body?

We know that the *luz* receives sustenance only from food that is eaten on *motza'ei Shabbos*. As the *Mishnah Berurah* states, this is one of the reasons behind the custom of the *melaveh malkah* meal. We also mentioned in the main text that the need for death was created only when Adam HaRishon ate from the Tree of Knowledge. Man must die in order to repair the damage Adam caused to his body and the creation. It is clear that when Adam ate from the tree, each and every part of his body was harmed by the fruit of the Tree of Knowledge. But there was one exception. Since Adam ate from the tree on *erev Shabbos*, a time when the *luz* is not receiving nourishment from eaten foods, it was not damaged by the fruit. Therefore, it does not need to go through the destruction and re-making that the rest of the body must experience.

In essence, the *luz* is the single part of us that exists as it was meant to be created — immortal. It is this piece that God will use to activate the resurrection.

> Our predecessors stated that man has a small bone that is called the *"naschui."* This bone remains intact in the grave until the time of the resurrection, even after the rest of the bones have decomposed. This bone does not receive sustenance from any food except the *melaveh malkah* meal.
>
> (*Mishnah Berurah*, vol. 3, 300:2)

27. Although most opinions — and certainly the simple meaning of Rav Katina's statement — suggest that the thousand years of destruction will be actual, physical destruction, there are *Rishonim* who disagree with this interpretation.

The Meiri explains that Rav Katina was referring, not to physical destruction, but to the cataclysmic troubles that will befall the world. According to this, the thousand years refers to the sixth millennium rather than the seventh, most of which has already past.

> "And one thousand [years] of destruction" (*Sanhedrin* 97a) — according to my understanding, this refers to one of the first six, hinting at the great troubles and confusion that are designated for the sixth millennium, according to the tradition of the Sages. It does not refer to a renewal of religion or the [physical] destruction of the world....
>
> (*Meiri*, Introduction to *Avos*)

The Rambam offers another interesting angle. He explains that even if Rav Katina's statement is meant to be taken literally, Rav

Katina's opinion was not accepted by the other Sages.

Furthermore, it is the statement of a lone opinion....

(Rambam, *Moreh Nevuchim* 2:29)

The Rashba, quoted in the notes to the main text, disagrees with the Rambam. He explains that since we find none of the Sages disagreeing directly with Rav Katina, we can assume that his opinion was the accepted one.

Glossary

Abarbanel — Rabbi Don Yitzchak Abarbanel (1437–1508), a philosopher, statesman, and leader of Spanish Jewry. His literary output was voluminous, including biblical commentary, philosophy, and works concerning the messianic era.

Acharonim — Literally, "later ones," referring to the Sages that followed the *Rishonim*, from the sixteenth century onward.

aggadic — Related to non-halachic material in the Talmud.

alav hashalom — Literally, "Peace upon him," i.e., "May he rest in peace."

Amora (pl.: Amoraim) — Talmudic Sage; the collective authors of the Gemara who lived from approximately 200–500 C.E.

Avos — The patriarchs, Avraham, Yitzchak, and Yaakov.

ba'al habayis — Layman.

Bavel — Babylonia.

Beis HaMikdash — Holy Temple in Jerusalem, destroyed by the Romans in the year 70 C.E.

beis midrash — Study hall where Torah is learned.

Chazal — Acronym for *"Chachomim zichronam livrachah* — our Sages, of blessed memory," referring to the Talmudic Sages.

chesed — Kind-heartedness; giving to others.

Eretz Yisrael — Land of Israel.

erev Shabbos — Sabbath eve.

erev yom tov — Eve of a Jewish festival.

gadol (pl.: gedolim) — Great person; leader of the Jewish people.

Gaon (pl.: Geonim) — The head of a Babylonian YESHIVAH; these Sages lived from approximately the sixth to the tenth centuries.

Gemara — The portions of the Talmud that explain and elaborate on the MISHNAH.

ger — Convert to Judaism.

heter — Legal permission.

Kesuvim — Writings; the third section of the Bible.

Kohen — Priests, descended from Aaron, brother of Moses.

Levi — A descendant of Levi, the son of Jacob.

Maharal — Rabbi Yehudah Loewe ben Betzalel (1526–1609), an important Jewish thinker. He was a prolific author, whose works encompass all areas of the Torah.

Midrash — Collection of homiletic interpretations of the Scriptures by the Sages of the MISHNAH.

Mishnah — The Tannaic code of Torah law compiled by Rabbi Yehudah HaNasi.

nachas — Pleasure; usually associated with the achievements of a child or student.

navi (pl.: nevi'im) — Prophet.

navi — Prophets; the second section of the Bible.

parsah — Unit of distance equal to approximately 2.7 miles.

posek (pl.: poskim) — Rabbinic authority on Jewish law.

Rambam — Maimonides; Rabbi Moses the son of Maimon (1135–1204), one of the leading Torah authorities and philosophers.

Ramban — Nachmanides; Rabbi Moses the son of Nachman (1194–1270), one of the leading commentators on the Torah and Talmud.

Ramchal — Rabbi Moshe Chaim Luzzato (1707–1746), one of the foremost mystical thinkers and author of works such as *Derech Hashem* and *Mesilas Yesharim*.

rebbetzin — Wife of a rabbi.

Rishonim — Literally, "early ones," referring to the Sages of approximately the eleventh to the fifteenth centuries.

ruach hakodesh — Divine inspiration, akin to prophecy in character, though of a lower stature.

Sanhedrin — The seventy-two-member legislative body that had jurisdiction over all religious matters in Eretz Yisrael during the Second Temple period.

sefer (pl.: sefarim) — Book; holy book.

Shabbos — Sabbath; the Jewish day of rest.

shemittah — Sabbatical year, which falls out one year in every seven, when all land in Eretz Yisrael is left fallow.

shlita — Acronym for *"sheyichyeh l'chaim tovim va'aruchim* — may he live a good, long life," often said after mentioning the name of a righteous person.

talmid (pl.: talmidim) — Student of Torah.

talmid chacham — Torah scholar.

Tanach — Acronym for Torah, *Nevi'im, Kesuvim* — the Torah, Prophets, and Writings — the three sections of the Bible.

Tanna (pl.: Tannaim) — Mishnaic Sages; the seven generations from Hillel to Rabbi Yehudah HaNasi, around 25 B.C.E.–200 C.E.

Yerushalayim — Jerusalem.

yeshivah — Torah institution.

yom tov — Jewish festival.

yovel — Jubilee year.

zocheh — He will merit.

Source Index

Torah

Nevi'im and Kesuvim

Chazal

GEMARA

MIDRASH

Primary Sources from the Geonim and Rishonim

Primary Sources from Acharonim

Subject Index